strategy+business

MAKE
OR BREAK

D0980598

How Manufacturers Can Leap from Decline to Revitalization

KAJ GRICHNIK
CONRAD WINKLER
WITH JEFFREY ROTHFEDER

McGraw Hill

New York   Chicago   San Francisco   Lisbon   London
Madrid   Mexico City   Milan   New Delhi   San Juan
Seoul   Singapore   Sydney   Toronto

1 2 3 4 5 6 7 8 9 0 DOC/DOC 0 9 8

ISBN 978-0-07-150830-8
MHID   0-07-150830-9

Design by Lee Fukui and Mauna Eichner

McGraw-Hill books are available at special quantity discounts to use as premiums and sales promotions, or for use in corporate training programs. To contact a representative please visit the Con-tact Us pages at www.mhprofessional.com.

This book is printed on acid-free paper.

CONTENTS

1

THE CROSSROADS

THERE'S NOTHING conventional about Zara's clothes—or about the way the company goes about making them. On its way to becoming one of the world's most successful retail fashion houses, Zara, a division of Spain's Inditex Group, has created a manufacturing process that deftly takes into account fast-paced global trends, cutting-edge business practices, and finicky consumer preferences. In so doing, Zara often finds itself sewing against the grain.

Zara divides its product lines into three categories. "Classic" garments change infrequently. For these garments, the company, like virtually all clothing makers, outsources its manufacturing to countries like Sri Lanka and Malaysia, where wages are low. "Fashion" clothes are seasonal; Zara produces these at its own factories and suppliers in Europe. "Trend" clothes are redesigned at rapid-fire speed in response to the latest tastes; they may stay in retail stores for as little as two weeks. Made in specialized high-speed factories owned either by Zara or by vendor partners, these trend clothes account for about half of the company's volume.

In dividing its manufacturing universe into three parts, Zara's goal is not to produce items at the cheapest price, but to produce the items that best satisfy, at any given moment, the tastes and needs of the consumers who walk through the doors of its retail stores. Because its clothes match consumer tastes so closely, Zara sells as much as 80 percent of its products at full price—about twice the industry average. This extra margin, in turn, allows the company to keep its investment in operations—in its factories and supply chain, its distribution channels and technologies—at the forefront of its industry.

Rather than farm out manufacturing to whoever can make clothing least expensively, Zara designed its manufacturing system around quality, speed, and consumer behavior. For its fashion and trend lines, the production cycle is kept short and intensely responsive to information gathered from retail stores—about which products shoppers buy, what they try on, whether they have problems with zippers or fit, and what they request. Zara's rapid-fire designers can produce a new garment in response to consumer demand within a few weeks, put it out in the trend line, and then—if consumer interest so dictates—move it to one of the other, slower-moving product lines. Exhibit 1-1 shows workers at Zara's factory for trend clothing in Arteixo, Spain, laying out patterns generated by computers at the direction of the company's 200 in-house designers, who work across the street. The interchange

EXHIBIT 1-1   ZARA BEHIND THE SCENES

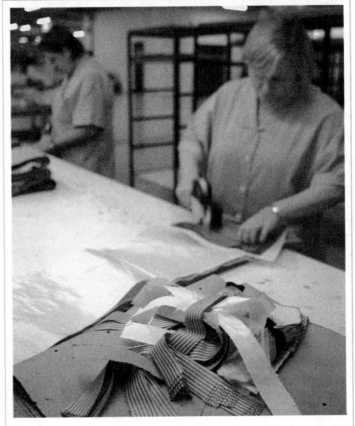

Photo courtesy of Inditex

among data from the store, decisions made by the design-ers, fabrication, and distribution is nearly seamless—and is improving all the time.

This ability to respond quickly avoids markdowns and more than compensates for any added manufacturing and distribution costs. Compared to an unnamed but real spe-cialty retailer (Exhibit 1-2), Zara compensates for its 15 percent lower list prices and higher production costs in two ways: its gross margin dollars are actually 55 percent greater because it does not need to discount; and it sells approximately 20 percent more units per square foot. It accomplishes this through its farsighted manufacturing practices, which are integrated tightly with knowledge about its customers. As a result of Zara's manufacturing operations, its parent company, Inditex, has been able to report a steady stream of earnings gains at a time when many other clothing manufacturers are struggling with shrinking profit margins.

Zara stands out because its leaders see something that many companies are too myopic to recognize: the prospects for manufacturing have never been better. Innovation is rampant, capital is available for experimentation, global markets with billions of consumers are opening their doors to new and existing products, technological changes have enabled new types of materials and processes, and the standard of living for people in established and developing economies is steadily improving. Indeed, prowess in operations and fabrication is a critical platform upon which leading companies can still build their next wave of success—and some of them will.

The only problem is that comparatively few companies are behaving as if they're entering a golden age for manufacturing. Indeed, all these signs of a potentially bright future have appeared at the nadir of manufacturing's perceived influence and impact on the world of business. It is difficult to pinpoint the precise moment that this happened, but at some point in the latter part of the twentieth century, business leaders in general, and even manufacturers themselves, seem to have lost respect for manufacturing.

EXHIBIT 1-2 ZARA'S UNIQUE VALUE PROPOSITION

SPECIALTY RETAILER

$100
Regular
price

Markdown

$30
Cost of
goods

UNITS PER SQUARE FOOT

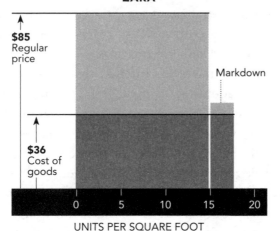

ZARA

$85
Regular
price

Markdown

$36
Cost of
goods

UNITS PER SQUARE FOOT

Source: Booz Allen Hamilton analysis

This loss of respect is unfortunate, even puzzling, because most companies are still producers of goods, even in an Internet age. They depend on the manufacturing function, and they are almost certainly going to be preoccupied with manufacturing processes and performance in the coming years.

At the same time, the manufacturing function will face a formidable mix of challenges during the next 20 years. These include shortages of energy and raw materials, stricter environmental regulations, a wild expansion in product complexity and variety, outdated infrastructures, and a dearth of motivated and capable personnel. It is hard to see how manufacturing units can cope with this cocktail of global challenges if they are treated as the weakest link in their companies.

In short, producers of goods—those companies that rely partly on manufacturing for their livelihood—stand at a crossroads today. And since both social welfare and national economies depend for their vitality on a healthy manufacturing sector, so do the rest of us. All of the elements that could launch a revival of manufacturing are at hand, and manufacturers can take that path, boldly and deliberately adopting the managerial and technological practices—some old, some new—that will allow them to thrive, even while facing intensifying pressures. But unfortunately, many manufacturers have chosen a path that leads directly away from this exciting series of possibilities. If they continue in that vein, unable or unwilling to generate solutions to the problems facing them, we may see not just companies, but whole industries wither. Not just in the Rust Belts of industrialized nations, but around the world, manufacturers will doom themselves to decline, and in some cases extinction.

That's why this inquiry into manufacturing's future is titled *Make or Break*. It explores whether manufacturing will break (continue to suffer irreparable losses) or whether it will make an invaluable contribution to fulfilling corporate aspirations. Neither future is preordained, either at the macroeconomic level of a country or at the micro level of an individual firm. To "make or break" is the most critical choice facing every manufacturing leader.

FACING CHOICES

To many observers in this world of financial competition and fervent cost cutting, the idea of basing business success on production prowess may seem quaint and passé. But a handful of the world's most successful companies would most strongly disagree. Indeed, the most attractive future for manufacturers—and for manufacturing itself— is inevitably foreshadowed in the stories of those leading companies that have been farsighted enough to view their factories and supply chains (and the human and technological capabilities embedded in them) as strategic assets.

These companies include proud manufacturers like Procter & Gamble, which has long been a pioneer of novel factory-floor environments. P&G began its innovative participative shop-floor approach in the 1960s, letting shop-floor employees not just manage their work, but lay out the flow of machinery and sometimes design the machines. In one celebrated case at a P&G plant in Lima,

Ohio, a team of shop-floor "technicians," as hourly workers were called, concocted a machine for properly positioning detergent bottles on the assembly line—a mechanical feat that professional engineers had said was impossible. Today, this focus on process innovation on the factory floor is a critical part of P&G's strategy. In P&G's simple but compelling logic, product innovation is a fragile advantage (and easily copied through reverse engineering), while process innovation is much more robust and long-lasting. Hence, investments in manufacturing come more naturally to P&G and have led to truly differentiated processes for a wide variety of products.

Similarly, effective approaches to the management of operations can be found among such manufacturers as the packaging giant Tetra Pak, the toy manufacturer Lego, the aircraft maker Boeing, the Chinese appliance juggernaut Haier, and arguably the most innovative producer on the planet, Toyota. Perhaps the most striking characteristic of these companies is that they see their success over the next few years as being determined by their decisions about manufacturing, and not just by their sales, marketing, or M&A initiatives.

That determination to keep the manufacturing function vital will deliver a hard-won competitive advantage for companies that have the vision to see it. Extracting real and sustainable value from manufacturing requires extraordinary skills. And even the most capable companies have to work extremely hard to keep their edge. Toyota, for instance, is investing massive amounts of money to reinvigorate the continuous improvement approaches of its older plants after it discovered that newly established locations were outperforming them.

We wrote this book to offer global business professionals a deeper understanding of the opportunities for manufacturing along with the perils they may face and the potential for overcoming them. Our premise is that failure to pay appropriate attention to this function will not be sustainable for companies much longer. Even if there is currently a glut of product on the market, the success of firms like P&G and Toyota has shown that the demand for quality, reliability, and longevity is real and increasing. In that context, the future of manufacturing is embedded in a host of serious questions, including these: What price will economies and societies pay for allowing the manufacturing work environment to slip so precipitously? How can a company credibly sell products that its employees hate making? Will older industrial economies ever be great manufacturers again? If so, how?

To start answering those questions, we look at the wide range of specific trends that will affect manufacturing—and at the evolution of new production methods, techniques, philosophies, and strategies that could positively influence the performance of industry and improve global economic, environmental, and social conditions. We describe how current and future trends are conspiring to alter the dynamics of manufacturing, and we explain how manufacturers can transform themselves to achieve success in a difficult landscape.

The prospects for manufacturing are as great as they are because the challenges are so difficult. When companies face their current realities squarely and without flinching, the effort and the cost to produce manufacturing value can have a huge potential payoff. But it will take deliberate, strategic dedication to realize that return. Listen to what

Ken Freeman, former CEO of Corning Glass, says about accomplishing this in a period of hypercompetition:

> Corning had invented color television glass, alongside RCA. But in the early 1990s, the television set business faced tough international competition, and Corning had reduced its exposure by creating a joint venture with Asahi Glass. Employees in the factories were very proud. They didn't buy the fact that customers were unhappy with Corning's quality and service. They simply denied that their products were anything but the best. The employees weren't hearing direct feedback from the customers. "You're the third CEO in five years," they said to me. "You're telling us the customers are going to walk away. We've outlasted the last two guys who told us that. Why should we believe you?"
>
> So I shut down the factory for nine days. I brought in customers to speak with all of our employees, from the factory utility workers to the head of manufacturing. I said to the customers, "You've got to tell my employees exactly what you told me—that if we think we can get by with poor quality, you will figure out a way to get by without having us as a supplier." And they did. The employees suddenly turned their chairs around and started listening more attentively to our customers. After that event they started coming together to improve product quality and service. Together, we turned that business around.

Today, Corning is the worldwide leader in the development, manufacture, and supply of LCD substrates, essential components for flat-panel TVs, desktop monitors, and notebook computers. In 2006, its display technologies business contributed 41 percent of the company's $5.1 billion in revenues.

If manufacturing is to fulfill its promise in the next few years, a variety of remarkable technologies, ideas, and shifts in attitude will be needed to break the boundaries of conventional practices. More direct connections between shop-floor employees and customers will be just one of them. Among many other possibilities, old fossilized plant footprints must become more nimble networks; confrontational labor relationships must evolve into constellations of joint interests; outmoded supply chains must be transformed into clearly defined, mutually beneficial partnerships; fabrication techniques must be revitalized through the use of new materials and machinery; stolid, aging factories must be retrofitted to become showcases of lean manufacturing. Looking farther ahead, edgy concepts such as instant manufacturing and biomimicry (fabrication based on principles derived from nature) must be tested and adopted where appropriate. In a period of dematerialization, of service industries and product fatigue, of globalization, environmental concerns, and dwindling supplies of raw materials and energy, these methods will allow innovative manufacturers to navigate the coming maelstrom.

NATURE'S INSPIRATION

Janine Benyus, author of *Biomimicry,* is one of several innovative thinkers who are helping to conceive of ways in which manufacturing and materials could evolve during the next few decades. The Biomimicry Guild, which Benyus cofounded, fosters approaches that consciously emulate the patterns, designs, and strategies of plants, animals, and ecosystems in manufacturing environments. In a 2006 interview conducted by *strategy + business* editor Amy Bernstein, she described the impact that this approach could have on manufacturing capabilities:

> The traditional processes for turning materials into finished products are incredibly wasteful and polluting. They're called "heat, beat, and treat": you start with a bulk material, carve it down, heat it up, beat it with enormous pressure, and treat it with chemicals. What you get is 96 percent waste, 4 percent product.
>
> Researchers are now looking at the processes that nature uses to make its materials—from ceramics like shell, bone, and teeth to the soft and yet amazingly durable materials like spider silk—to identify common principles. There are several primary differences. First, life does its manufacturing in or near its own body, so its methods have to be life-friendly. A spider spins its silk "on board." It can't take a chance with "heat, beat, and treat." It uses little energy; there's no waste and no hazardous byproduct. Second, nature conducts its chemistry in water. We conduct industrial chemistry in solvents like sulfuric acid. Third, our manufacturing processes use all the elements in the periodic table—even the toxic ones—and we use crude, brute-force recipes. But life uses a subset of

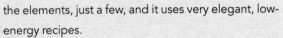

the elements, just a few, and it uses very elegant, low-energy recipes.

One of the problems with "heat, beat, and treat" is that it tends to produce brittle materials that crack or break easily. The abalone shell, by contrast, is a model of flexibility and resilience . . . [and] twice as durable as the ceramics we use in jet engines.

One major roadblock is that translating the natural self-assembly process into an industrial process is very challenging. However, it is being done in a variety of places, like the Sandia National Laboratories at Albuquerque, where Jeff Brinker [a materials scientist at Sandia and the University of New Mexico] is creating self-assembling materials. He's working on optically clear glass that could be used in windshields for cars—basically, liquefied beach sand [and] a detergent kind of molecule that herds the organic material together into layers. It's a very, very tough material—seven times tougher than our windshields.

Another promising technique is solid free-form fabrication, also called rapid prototyping, which builds three-dimensional objects layer by layer without any need for molding or shaping. Right now, it's being used for product prototyping in all kinds of engineering and design studios, but some researchers are looking at how to scale the technique up to "print" a whole house. A CAD program would instruct a crane to lay down layer after layer of cement, or whatever building material you'd use, to build walls. Self-assembly is a huge paradigm shift, but it's the future of manufacturing.

MANUFACTURING'S
LONG EBB TIDE

The most innovative and committed manufacturers today are swimming against the tide of a half-century of history. The early industrial era was a wild epoch of breathtaking progress in production systems and factory design. But this ended, more or less, in the mid-1960s, when the typical Western industrial company retreated into stasis. As financial conglomeration, not manufacturing, came to be seen as more of a growth driver, managers began to treat their manufacturing operations as cost centers—to be cut back first when times got tight. Consequently, in the 1970s, when Western manufacturers faced their first real global challenge from a wave of more efficient, higher-quality, and lower-cost Asian competition, old-line industrial executives were often at a loss for how to respond to the changed landscape. Many of them reacted by doing little and hoping for the best.

In the 1980s, a new paradigm emerged from Japanese manufacturers in the guise of streamlined assembly processes and methods for capturing quality gains. Known as the "quality movement" and later as "lean production," it was led by experts in statistical process control, including some Americans, like W. Edwards Deming and Joseph Juran, who had been virtually ignored in their home country for years. Lean production systems and exotic tools like kaizen (continuous improvement practice), poka-yoke (mistake-proof product and process designs), kanban (production line signals to regulate the flow of work), and the heijunka box (a type of production scheduling) became all the rage. No self-respecting manufacturer could ignore the new possibilities that these fresh ideas offered. Western companies freely tried to copy these approaches, studying companies like Toyota and Honda as if their playbooks were the Gospel.

Some business pundits predicted that there would be a manufacturing revolution built on Japanese breakthroughs in integrated production processes and advances in automation. It was predicted that manual labor in factories would be widely replaced by machines, creating "lights-out" facilities, and that lean production systems would yield double-digit productivity improvements, allowing Western manufacturers to fend off low-cost competition.

Many large companies started in-house programs to develop optimum production approaches. By the 1990s, university programs like the Leaders for Manufacturing (LFM) program at the Massachusetts Institute of Technology, the Master of Management in Manufacturing (MMM) at Northwestern University, and the Cambridge University Institute for Manufacturing were established to train the best and brightest for manufacturing excellence. Business publications featured more articles about manufacturing than ever before. The factories of the future, they confidently proclaimed, were ready for dramatic change.

Some of these predictions were borne out in the West—but in only a few plants, and ironically many of those were new Japanese-owned factories, such as Nissan and Toyota plants in the United States and England. The photograph in Exhibit 1-3, taken at the Toyota Technical Skills Academy in Toyota City, Japan (a high school for future

EXHIBIT 1-3 TOYOTA'S ACADEMY

Source: Ko Sasaki/*The New York Times*/Redux

factory leaders) depicts a session related to the company's ongoing efforts to involve people in reducing maintenance costs by improving day-by-day practices.

Despite its reputation in the business press, lean production never quite took hold at many Western manufacturers. Few manufacturers had the knowledge and the will to retrofit older "brownfield" manufacturing plants; even fewer had the funds and the corporate freedom to open brand-new "greenfield" locations with lean practices embedded from the start. Observations of manufacturing plants in a variety of industries in the United States and the European Union show that far fewer than 10 percent of the companies in any of these industries demonstrate mastery of lean production techniques (see Exhibit 1-4). Typically, the lack of lean success in the remaining 90 percent of companies is not due to lack of trying. Most companies have tried to embrace the concept in some fashion but failed—often more than once. The quality of manufactur-

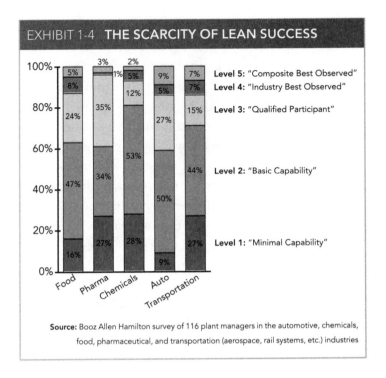

EXHIBIT 1-4 **THE SCARCITY OF LEAN SUCCESS**

Level 5: "Composite Best Observed"
Level 4: "Industry Best Observed"
Level 3: "Qualified Participant"
Level 2: "Basic Capability"
Level 1: "Minimal Capability"

Source: Booz Allen Hamilton survey of 116 plant managers in the automotive, chemicals, food, pharmaceutical, and transportation (aerospace, rail systems, etc.) industries

ing's future depends, in part, on how many companies can gravitate from the middle bands of the chart in Exhibit 1-4 up to the top.

Despite their initial enthusiasm for lean manufacturing systems, Western companies were unable to develop the rigorous internal discipline and learning processes that were required if these new approaches were to evolve within their operations. Instead, they anxiously implemented quick fixes and grew disenchanted when they realized that the commitment required to generate long-term returns was beyond the culture of their companies.

"Most Western companies have been simply unable to sustain the long and difficult process of understanding lean principles in their totality and then building their own capabilities using these principles," says Jeffrey Liker, director of the Japan Technology Management Program at the University of Michigan and author of *The Toyota Way: 14 Management Principles from the World's Greatest Manufacturer* (McGraw-Hill, 2003).

Frustrated by the meager gains from lean manufacturing, throughout the 1990s many Western companies began to wonder anew whether there was any value in manufacturing at all. Their doubts were buttressed by the new rigid economic value added (EVA) metrics that they adopted, which dictated that the cost of capital investment must be taken into account when calculating every aspect of corporate performance. With that approach, factories and production systems were often viewed as a poor use of capital. Consequently, a considerable number of companies began to give up even paying lip service to operations investment. Instead, they relegated manufacturing—even if it was arguably a core operation—to little more than a poor stepchild, a likely target for cost cutting or outsourcing.

Not surprisingly, throughout the past few decades, despite all the ballyhooed reorganizations and lean management efforts, factory productivity growth has been minimal. Between 1980 and 2006, for example, American manufacturers added 88 percent more capacity to their factory networks, but they failed to make any more productive use of it. Indeed, after 1998, capacity utilization actually fell, even though production accelerated! As Exhibit 1-5 shows, actual productivity gains are also smaller than the prevailing figures suggest when such factors as outsourcing, offshoring, the use of intermediary service providers, and the costs of inflation are taken into account.

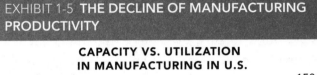

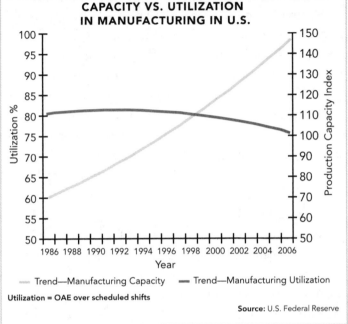

EXHIBIT 1-5 **THE DECLINE OF MANUFACTURING PRODUCTIVITY**

CAPACITY VS. UTILIZATION IN MANUFACTURING IN U.S.

Trend—Manufacturing Capacity   Trend—Manufacturing Utilization

Utilization = OAE over scheduled shifts

Source: U.S. Federal Reserve

Western manufacturing in the latter years of the twentieth century was symbolized by such sordid tales as the decline of the American company Sunbeam. After being acquired by Allegheny International, Sunbeam's manufacturing division was "starved of capital to update its factories and refresh its product line," as author John Byrne put it in the book *Chainsaw: The Notorious Career of Al Dunlap in the Era of Profit-at-Any-Price* (Collins, 2003). Then, cost-cutting turnaround guru Al Dunlap was named CEO in 1996, and manufacturing capacity suffered even more erosion. In an aggressive attempt to raise Sunbeam's share price, Dunlap wiped out factory operating expenditures. Typical of Dunlap's actions, according to Byrne, was replacing a high-quality, efficient hair-clipper plant in McMinnville, Tennessee, with a chaotic, poorly managed, unproductive new facility near Mexico City. Quality dropped; so did customer loyalty, and ultimately sales. Moving operations without maintaining differentiated quality was just one of the many ways that Dunlap's regime put manufacturing in a backseat and ultimately destroyed shareholder value. In the end, management had to massage the numbers to keep them looking healthy. Sunbeam's stock price plunged, and the company filed for bankruptcy protection in 2001.

Stories like Sunbeam's suggest why truly motivated plant communities are now few and far between and why few chief executives have emerged from the ranks of manufacturing managers. Dismissed for the lack of value it ostensibly brings to companies and increasingly rejected by the public at large as a rewarding source of employment (even in China today, workers are starting to prefer service over factory jobs), manufacturing has become nothing less than a second-class endeavor.

Will the rise of new industrial economies create a shift in direction? Since 2001, there has been a significant increase in manufacturing capital investment from the West in Asia and Eastern Europe. These plants are mainly being established to meet strong local demand for new products, especially in the case of Asia. Yet, in the headlong rush to build up capacity in those lower-cost regions, most companies—both domestic and foreign—have been able to ignore the imperative of change. They have basically gone about manufacturing in the same way they always have.

Chinese greenfield plants almost never take advantage of the lessons learned by their Japanese and Western predecessors—for example, that the best way to ensure the success of lean systems is to install them at the beginning, even before the factory doors open.

Indeed, while manufacturing output in China totaled about 60 percent of that in the United States in 2006, the market for lean trainers and specialists there is barely 4 percent of that in the West. In the end, as quality, logistics, and cost fragility inevitably become higher priorities for manufacturers in low-cost nations, they too will be forced to revamp their factory networks and will face the barriers inherent in adding improved production techniques to existing operations. Indeed, this is already beginning to happen.

MANUFACTURING MYOPIA

In the 1960s, Harvard Business School's Theodore Levitt coined the concept of "marketing myopia." Professor Levitt argued that companies made themselves vulnerable when they defined their brands too narrowly. Railroads are not in the passenger-train business, he argued; they're in the transportation industry. But failing to realize that, railroads never considered trying to compete against cars, trucks, airplanes, and even the telephone, and thus they ceded a huge potential market to other companies that they never perceived as rivals. Today, myopia is even more prevalent in manufacturing than it was in marketing four decades ago.

> Like marketing myopia, manufacturing myopia is caused by functional isolation; it is the inevitable outcome of keeping manufacturing decisions contained at the plant level, with little or no connection to companywide strategies. As the factories and supply chain overseas are cut off from the rest of the executive decision makers, the manufacturing focus grows narrower, and overall competence atrophies. This compels companies to cut costs even more blindly and irresponsibly, often by setting companywide targets determined by financial fiat rather than by competitive or customer insights.

Perhaps the best way to understand the state of manufacturing management is to compare the chief manufacturing officer to the technician who presides over the engine room of a cruise ship. That, at least, is the view of Michel Lurquin, the manufacturing chief at the biopharmaceutical firm UCB Group. "If everything goes well," says Lurquin, "few staff or passengers will be interested. But if the engine fails, it can totally ruin the cruise."

THE HEART OF THE ECONOMY

At one time, manufacturing was the very heart of the economy in most developed countries. Being able to make products and ship them around the world to waiting markets was the primary way in which the United States and many European nations established employment and purchasing power for a vast middle class at home. This also ensured a steady flow of income onto Treasury balance sheets.

Today, with so many companies blind to the value of manufacturing, and with so many manufacturing jobs being sent offshore or ceded to low-cost competitors, there is a distinct possibility that more than a few Western nations will lose their base as producers. Dominated by service industries, they will remain consumers of manufactured goods. As a consequence, these countries may well lose their edge in technology and innovation and their geopolitical economic leverage—aspects of national well-being that have traditionally been fostered by a strong manufacturing sector.

The consequences of the decline in manufacturing are hard to ignore. By mid-2007 manufacturing employment in the United States had fallen to 14.1 million, a drop-off of more than 3 million in 10 years and a level not seen since the 1950s. Meanwhile, the U.S. trade deficit stood at a historically high 5 percent of gross domestic product (GDP), while foreign debt had reached a massive 25 percent of GDP. The combination of all of these elements, never experienced before, leads some experts to believe that if the manufacturing base continues to weaken, the United States and many European Union nations will suffer accelerated deterioration in their dominant status among world economies, and their citizens will have to accept a worsening of their standards of living.

Clearly, a host of variables—many of them unknown—will determine how the hemorrhaging of the manufacturing base in developed nations would ultimately affect those nations. But one thing is certain in virtually every imaginable scenario: manufacturing is a valuable asset. If the world stands at a crossroads for manufacturing, there are several plausible outcomes. One is a future in which, after shrinking temporarily, manufacturing in developed nations reinvents itself and rebounds. In another scenario, manufacturing continues to gravitate to low-cost countries whenever it can. In a third outcome, some companies learn to play the manufacturing game well, while others do not, and the winners become truly global companies that build robust economies in a distributed fashion around the planet. Whatever happens, one thing is certain: the footprint of manufacturing will play an immensely important role in plotting the geopolitical and economic map for generations to come.

With so much at stake, governments can still have a significant say in the future of manufacturing. Monetary policy, trade initiatives, health-care programs, labor laws, and tax regulations can be designed to fortify a nation's industrial base—and some countries appear to be taking advantage of this. In 2005, the French government identified a series of critical industries, including aerospace, nuclear power, and pharmaceuticals, in which takeovers would be prevented. The U.S. Congress is currently considering a one-year depreciation schedule for capital investment, which would be a very helpful move. If manufacturing conditions worsen, some nations may move toward protectionist trade policies, despite their ill effects on economic growth.

Within companies, manufacturing remains one of the great underused and unrecognized sources of competitive advantage and share value. By seizing this opportunity, some business heroes will be made—even if they aren't yet recognized today. One probable arena for this will be intellectual property; manufacturing expertise represents the first defense against rivals and pirates who would copy success. It is arguably more difficult to emulate process innovation than product innovation, which can be reverse engineered. Even in industries such as pharmaceuticals, where product innovation is imperative, a growing number of cases have emerged in which products are defended through process patents. As more and more products are designed with unique production processes that make them performance- and price-competitive, manufacturing innovation will be increasingly valued.

> **PROCTER & GAMBLE** is one of the few companies in the fast-moving consumer goods industry that considers factory equipment design and development to be core strengths. For example, P&G's Babycare "enterprise technology" lines produce hundreds more diapers per minute than off-the-shelf manufacturing technology can, and its Cascade brand dishwashing detergent product lines are orders of magnitude faster than those of its main competitors—a fact that has consistently kept P&G among the top sellers in these product segments.

Other capabilities will also grow among leading-edge manufacturing firms—for example, the ability to beat competitors' response times by linking factory operations seamlessly into the supply chain. One aerospace company recently rebuilt its domestic factory system when it realized that it had to be able to meet its customers' design changes promptly—often something as simple as the location of holes drilled in basic floor panels for airplane cabins. This allowed it to achieve a rapid response that long-distance factories in low-cost nations simply could not match.

And general manufacturing capability may regain its power to instill confidence in shareholders and consumers. Even today, in the eyes of many customers, companies that manufacture their own products make them with more care and quality than those that farm out the work. Indeed, the public reaction to companies that outsource core brands can be harsh—especially when most people initially believed they didn't do so. Lowenbrau failed in the U.S. market after it became known that the beer wasn't German after all, but instead was made in America by a contractor. By contrast, Harley-Davidson continues to thrive in part because of its decision to manufacture its motorcycles mostly in-house in the United States. Harley-Davidson's resulting "Made in America" brand image is so strong today that consumers don't care if its accessories and ancillary merchandise, such as clothing, are produced overseas by contractors; those operations are peripheral to the brand image of Harley-Davidson's primary products.

Why, given the dismal track record of the past few years, is there suddenly reason to hope that manufacturing can regain its rightful stature as the heart of the industrial economy? It's not that senior leaders in manufacturing companies are becoming more enlightened en masse. Instead, the pressures that will force them to change their practices are finally intensifying past a threshold point. The choice that they are being offered—to make or break— is becoming ever more strident.

When you encounter an unfamiliar crossroads, the first thing you look for is a signpost. Many manufacturers are looking for exactly that kind of guidance today. Some will indeed decline, including some of the best-known producers of goods in industrial history. But some manufacturers, and not only those located in low-cost labor centers or Asian markets, will evolve. We explore their possible avenues for evolution in this book. They will find their own combinations of the innovative technologies, ideas, and attitudes needed to succeed at manufacturing. These companies will, sooner or later, shape a renaissance in manufacturing. They must; the cost of manufacturing faltering is too great—for the companies themselves, and for the rest of us as workers, consumers, and citizens.

For notes and resources visit our Web site:
www.businessfuture.com

2

POWERFUL
CHALLENGES

IN THE ARENA of manufacturing, the old adage, "What doesn't kill you, makes you stronger," is about to be tested. For while the manufacturing function is weaker in many companies than it has ever been before—in both capabilities and influence—it is also facing some of the most daunting challenges in business history.

The mainstream business press in the Western nations, at least, tends to emphasize only one of these challenges: competition from emerging nations with low-cost labor pools and burgeoning offshore enterprises. However, research suggests that low-cost labor is just one of the serious set of pressures that will test the manufacturing function in industries around the world during the next two decades.

Among the other pressing concerns that manufacturers must learn to navigate: shortages of materials and

EXHIBIT 2-1 EIGHT CHALLENGES OF MANUFACTURING

Competition   Environmental

Pressures

Workforce

New Customers

Shortages — The Manufacturing Function — Demand

Material

Expanding Variety

Conflict

Labor   Management

Source: Booz Allen Hamilton

labor; explosive growth in demand for products, especially in emerging markets; the increasing consumer thirst for items that closely match individual preferences; a new set of environmental imperatives against which all manufacturers will be judged; a congested commercial landscape full of new competitors; and for many unfortunate companies, continued labor conflicts and lack of support for the manufacturing function from inside their own organizations (see Exhibit 2-1).

Some of these challenges have been present in some industries for many years and others are new; but all of them are growing in intensity and becoming global. The more universal of these challenges include tense labor relationships, conflicts about the value of manufacturing within companies, and the surge in product variety. Meeting the demand for variety has always been difficult for manufacturers, but now a greater number than ever before of alternatives and "options" are available for products ranging from toothpaste to automobiles. Some challenges can affect particular regions or industries with particular intensity: In the automotive sector, these include unprecedented levels of competition, new environmental and energy issues, and materials shortages. In pharmaceuticals, they include growing levels of complexity, resulting from escalating levels of packaging and product customization. But as we shall see, the challenges are interrelated. Every industrial and consumer-product sector will have to deal with most (or all) of them during the next 10 to 20 years.

Manufacturing leaders exist in a gritty, hard-boiled corporate culture, and the enormity of these challenges helps explain why. It's easiest to be stoic about them, to try to keep moving as if leaning into a stiff wind, and to be skeptical about any longer-term aspirations. "How can you expect us to look to the future?" they ask. "Consider our present—commodity competitors! angry labor unions! rising steel prices!"

And it's true: none of these obstacles will disappear on their own. But consider: are these really challenges to manufacturing per se? Or are they challenges to the way that manufacturing is currently organized and practiced?

As we show later in this book, the way that manufacturing responds to these issues will make a tremendous difference. The quality and intensity of the response over time, and the degree to which manufacturing rises to the overall challenge of reinventing itself, will ultimately shape the structure of business around the world.

ARE CHALLENGES GOOD OR BAD?

In *The Art of the Long View* (Doubleday, 1991), scenario planning expert Peter Schwartz describes how Japanese resilience in the face of adversity is arguably that nation's ". . . greatest asset in the modern world. In 1973, the United States and Japan were hit with the same challenge: a quadrupling of oil prices." To Schwartz, the Americans responded first with bravado ("This is temporary; we will surely win") and then with capitulation: within a year, the United States was importing half its oil. But Japan took a different tack: ". . . completely rebuilding its capital infrastructure to become the most energy-efficient economy in the world." If the United States had been able to reduce energy usage to a similar degree, one can imagine a different economic and political situation in the United States today.

Such is the benefit of a challenge for those who have the wherewithal and resourcefulness to rise to it. Once they make it through the period of crisis, they find a host of unexpected benefits, both in the new capabilities they gain and in the links they forge along the way with allies and new partners. And, as with Japan and energy efficiency, the decisions made during a challenge can make all the difference in later years.

1. MATERIAL SHORTAGES

Since World War II, and today more than ever, companies face growing shortages in key raw materials, everything from once commonplace supplies, such as steel and aluminum, to high-value elements such as gold, silver, copper, and platinum. Even recycled materials are increasingly scarce. In general, these shortages are due primarily to the inability of mining and processing facilities to keep up with ballooning economic growth in emerging countries like China, India, and Brazil. This situation will continue to deteriorate over the long term as raw materials become depleted in the face of heightened demand.

Copper is an apt example. Many futurists had long assumed that the demand for copper, as well as other metals, would decline as companies developed new synthetic materials. But a team of researchers at Yale University found that the need for copper around the world hit record highs in the first years of the twenty-first century. Indeed, according to the researchers' data, every last bit of copper still unmined, plus all of the copper currently in use, would be needed to bring undeveloped nations to the level of developed countries in power transmission, construction, automobiles, and weaponry. "Either the rest of the world can't live like the developed world or we need, as a society, to think more about the technology of providing these services with less intensive use of at least certain materials," says Thomas Graedel, Yale University Clifton R. Musser Professor of Industrial Ecology.

Silver, which will be increasingly needed for such critical innovations as solar cell production, faces a similar shortfall. Industrial silver usage levels grew by 6 percent in 2006 to a record 430 million ounces, after rising 11 percent the year before, according to the Silver Institute. This was the fifth consecutive year of rising demand that exceeded global GDP growth. Based on current consumption trends, the entire known mining reserves of silver could be depleted by 2023. To overcome this shortfall, the solar industry, which relies on silver in its equipment, has been working on product advances that use more abundantly available materials as substitutes.

The availability of steel depends, in turn, on the availability of iron ore—and that too is in short supply. Global steel production is expected to continue growing annually at 5 percent per year, at least through 2010, with the majority of growth coming from China. Chinese annual production of crude steel is expected to increase by 236 megatons by that year, ending up at an estimated total production volume of about 570 Mt. While China shifts from being a net importer of steel to a net exporter, with an estimated export volume of 60 Mt in 2007, suppliers of iron are consolidating. Currently, 60 percent of the global iron ore trading volume is generated by just three companies: CVRD Inco Limited, based in Brazil and Canada; the British/Australian Rio Tinto Group; and BHP Billiton, another Australia-based company. Because of its increased requirements for steel, China is gobbling up most of the available iron ore. Supplies of the other most important raw material for steel, coking coal, also are highly concentrated. Then there are elements, such as molybdenum, that are used as alloys in steel production (e.g., to improve the corrosion resistance and weldability of stainless steel). More than half the market share for steel alloys is held by just five top suppliers. In short, since access to cheap, reliable, and high-quality raw materials is the key ingredient for low-cost steel, the cost of steel will continue to rise.

Shortages in alloys may not be great in terms of absolute volume, but they can have a disproportionate impact because of their use in industrial equipment. For example, molybdenum is used in the making of steel rolls, fundamental machinery for hot-rolling mills. Indeed, more than 80 percent of the molybdenum used commercially is used for this application. Thus, even if iron and coking coal remain available, the molybdenum supply could become a constraint on steel production: the world production of molybdenum was only 359 million pounds in 2006; only five countries (the United States, Chile, China, Canada, and Peru) account for 93 percent of production; and the only major mining expansion underway for this metal will not be ready until at least 2009.

Some manufacturing companies are attempting to minimize or delay potential raw material shortages through vertical integration: hedging by buying the raw material supply. For example, Tenaris, a global specialty steel manufacturer, recently bought a then nonoperative Romanian steel plant primarily for its relatively vast reserve of scrap metal from dismantled factories and railways around the Black Sea, dating back to the time when the country was a Soviet satellite. In similar fashion, carbon composites companies such as SGL Carbon, Hexcel, and Carbon Lorraine are vying for access to upstream carbon manufacturing capacity. But even when these stopgap solutions help mitigate shortages, they don't have any effect on long-term availability. In general, the quality of materials today often falls below the standards manufacturers are used to working with. Smaller manufacturers, which don't have vast market clout, are particularly affected by this loss of quality.

Though not a material in the strict sense of the word, manufacturing equipment is also in short supply and is just as critical to the manufacturing process as raw materials. Lead times for delivery of new factory machines, which are produced by relatively fewer, mostly Western manufacturers, have increased dramatically in the past three years. This can result in a corresponding increase in the capabilities gap between early and late adopters of new technologies. For those who are waiting in line while their competition already has the latest equipment in place, the disadvantage can be stark.

For example, in optical manufacturing (making lenses for eyeglasses), a three-dimensional computer-controlled milling technology called "free-form" manufacturing has been one breakthrough in the last 10 years. Carving out the dimensions of the lens in this way enables both a product result more closely customized to the end-user's eye and a less expensive process (because a much less expensive lens "blank" can be used). Having slowly discovered the benefits of this equipment, the major optical manufacturers have now embraced it, causing a backlog of orders for free-form milling machines. Those who lagged in placing their orders may have a challenging next few years as they struggle to compete using older technology.

In one sense, this might seem like terrific news; companies are finally waking up to the advantages of investing in manufacturing innovation. But not everyone is waking up; the primary drivers in this recent demand are Indian and Chinese companies. Most of the other companies on the waiting lists for new machines seem to be content to catch up with established technologies and industrial machines. They are not clamoring to leapfrog past competitors or gain competitive advantage through the development of new industrial processes, and the providers of machine tools, with their growing backlogs, have little incentive to offer anything new, even if many established technologies are more than 50 or 60 years old.

Indeed while the machine builders struggle to fill orders for their most popular equipment, innovation may suffer even more. New processes and use of new materials are particularly dependent on new forms of industrial equipment. This can be an unwelcome reality, particularly in industries that already have lackluster records for production advances and breakthroughs.

Throughout most of human history, society has coped with shortages in two basic ways: adapting to deprivation or embracing innovation. It is not yet clear how severe the shortages affecting manufacturing will be—and despite the lack of appetite for innovation to date, it is not yet clear how the manufacturing industry will respond. But we suspect that those few companies that have consistently taken risks by investing in R&D on new manufacturing technology will reap greater benefits than most people expect. And those companies that maintained the status quo will need to invest heavily in order to catch up.

R&D intensity, spending as a percentage of sales, is often a good measure of the innovation activity of an industry, regardless of its size. Exhibit 2-2 illustrates lagging R&D spending by the industrials sector (whose largest

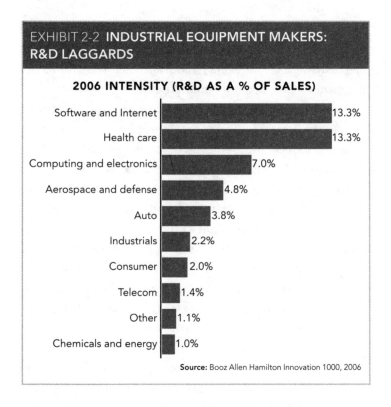

EXHIBIT 2-2 **INDUSTRIAL EQUIPMENT MAKERS: R&D LAGGARDS**

2006 INTENSITY (R&D AS A % OF SALES)

Industry	R&D as % of Sales
Software and Internet	13.3%
Health care	13.3%
Computing and electronics	7.0%
Aerospace and defense	4.8%
Auto	3.8%
Industrials	2.2%
Consumer	2.0%
Telecom	1.4%
Other	1.1%
Chemicals and energy	1.0%

Source: Booz Allen Hamilton Innovation 1000, 2006

segment is the purveyors of manufacturing equipment), compared to the industries it supplies, such as health-care, computer software, and aerospace. Only consumer products, telecom companies, and the chemical industry are investing less.

But that may change. Upstream industries like steel may also be forced to become more innovative as the shortages they face ripple out through the rest of the economy. Exhibit 2-3 shows the Number 5 blast furnace at the Tata Steel (formerly Corus) plant in Port Talbot, South Wales, United Kingdom.

EXHIBIT 2-3 A FUTURE CENTER FOR INNOVATION?

Photo courtesy http:..en.wikipedia.org/wiki/Image:Port_talbot_large.jpg

2. WORKFORCE SHORTAGES

In *Roger and Me,* Michael Moore's controversial 1989 movie about the decline of manufacturing in Flint, Michigan, there is an interview with a man whose job is to evict families that can't pay their rent. Throwing people out of their homes, he says, is much better than his former job, working on an automobile manufacturing assembly line. That job, he announces ruefully, "was like prison, man!"

How times had changed. As recently as the mid-1960s, in North America and Europe, a job in manufacturing was seen as a ticket to the middle class, the backbone of the economy, and a breadwinner's means of providing for his or her family. Then manufacturing became just a job that people took and kept out of necessity but left as soon as they could. By the time of *Roger and Me,* it was seen by many in the old industrial rust belts as a fate to be avoided altogether.

And many people still seem to see it that way—as a life sentence rather than an opportunity. That is one reason the manufacturing industries could face a serious shortfall in skilled workers.

But there are other reasons as well. One is the systematic neglect of in-house training in manufacturing, over many years and in many companies. In other words, there has been little effort to pass on the "institutional memory" of more experienced workers to the next generation. Meanwhile, as industrial processes grow more complex, the specialized knowledge required of a factory worker or manager grows, and no education system, no matter how well organized, can possibly compensate for the loss of on-the-job training by the previous generation.

Even manufacturing leaders, like Toyota and P&G, say the retention of staff and skills from one generation to the next is one of their toughest challenges. Toyota loses employees who find that their lean skills are highly valued by other companies, and P&G must cope with the outflux of operations talent to other functions within the firm. Executives in many other firms are also increasingly concerned about handing over decades of shop-floor experience from a stable older workforce with a commitment to long-term employment to younger generations that are far more transient and transactional in career terms. There are also demographic factors. The slowing birth rate in many parts of the world, and the vast number of imminent retirees, are taking their toll against the manufacturing workforce. In developed nations, population growth is forecast to sink to what demographers call a "replacement" fertility rate by 2030—meaning that just enough people will be born to replace those who die, with no net gains or losses in population. In subsequent decades, unless immigration makes up the difference, the total population in the industrialized world will probably begin to shrink.

Since life expectancy is also increasing, this constant population will almost certainly include an increasing proportion of aging and retired people—and thus a smaller number of potential factory workers. In Japan, the workforce is expected to shrink 20 percent by 2020. Ten years after that, Japan, Germany, the United Kingdom, and France will have only about two workers per retiree, down from a little over 3.5 in 2000, according to the U.S. Census Bureau's International Data Base. Conditions in the United States will be only slightly better, with workers per retiree falling from 4.65 to 2.67 between 2000 and 2030.

Finally, manufacturing is no longer the only game in town. Manufacturers must compete for their skilled workers, often for the first time, against other sectors and parts of the economy.

In many parts of the world, these relentless sociodemographic trends will likely result in a dearth of workers to fill factory jobs—especially where skilled manual labor is required. It will be an increasing challenge to find and retain enough people and the right people to make the items that growing global economies might demand. Moreover, even as workers will be more scarce for all types of jobs, fewer of the most talented people will be going into manufacturing. In fact, career track choices made by

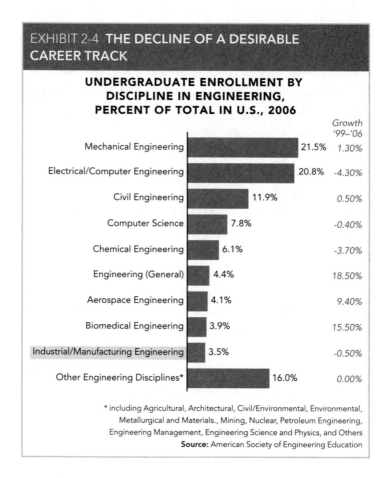

EXHIBIT 2-4 **THE DECLINE OF A DESIRABLE CAREER TRACK**

UNDERGRADUATE ENROLLMENT BY DISCIPLINE IN ENGINEERING, PERCENT OF TOTAL IN U.S., 2006

	Percent of Total	Growth '99–'06
Mechanical Engineering	21.5%	1.30%
Electrical/Computer Engineering	20.8%	-4.30%
Civil Engineering	11.9%	0.50%
Computer Science	7.8%	-0.40%
Chemical Engineering	6.1%	-3.70%
Engineering (General)	4.4%	18.50%
Aerospace Engineering	4.1%	9.40%
Biomedical Engineering	3.9%	15.50%
Industrial/Manufacturing Engineering	3.5%	-0.50%
Other Engineering Disciplines*	16.0%	0.00%

* including Agricultural, Architectural, Civil/Environmental, Environmental, Metallurgical and Materials., Mining, Nuclear, Petroleum Engineering, Engineering Management, Engineering Science and Physics, and Others
Source: American Society of Engineering Education

engineering students in the United States (Exhibit 2-4) show manufacturing and industrial engineering, the primary career track for manufacturing professionals, as the choice with the lowest attraction—and one of the minority that is trending down .

Some countries are already feeling the constraints of aging populations in which fewer young people choose to go into manufacturing, and these are by no means only rich, mature industrial nations. Even nations with lower

EXHIBIT 2-5   A CHINESE EMPLOYMENT WALL: MORE JOBS THAN SEEKERS

Source: Nelson Ching/*The New York Times*/Redux

labor costs and younger-than-average workers are likely to feel a significant labor pinch very soon—a possibility that already is of concern to many executives. For instance, when executives talk about the trends in China they worry about most, human capital shortages top the list, as shown in a January 2007 Economist Intelligence Unit Corporate Network Survey. A similar response was given by executives in Southeast Asia.

Exhibit 2-5, photographed in April 2006, shows a wall in Shenzhen, China, that is full of advertisements for manufacturing jobs but that is viewed by only a few people looking for work.

"Old Asia-hands may find it easy to understand why there is such concern," the *Economist* reported in August 2007. "The region's rapid economic growth has fished out the pool of available talent, they would say. But there is also a failure of education. Recent growth in many parts of Asia has been so great that it has rapidly transformed the type of skills needed by businesses. Schools and universities have been unable to keep up."

Faced with labor shortages in all parts of the globe, Western companies are already being forced to become much more creative about staffing manufacturing operations. Take the case of a medium-sized Northern Italian maker of forged tubes and fittings for utilities and chemical plants. This manufacturer enjoys revenue gains in double digits, primarily because of expanding sales in China. Not long ago, however, a change in product demand required that the company produce more welded products; and suddenly sales growth hit the wall. The manufacturer could not find enough trained people to weld, a somewhat unpleasant but skilled task. After more than a year of desperately searching for welders in its home region, the company decided to import a contingent of Romanian workers, a group the manufacturer discovered when buying used equipment there. In the not too distant future, however, even Romanian welders might prefer to work for, say, Starbucks, unless manufacturing employers of distinction can find ways to attract them.

Of course, companies can just attract employees by paying higher wage rates. But higher wages also end up making a company unable to compete with low-wage producers. As we'll see in subsequent chapters, some companies can do just as well competing for talent on the basis of distinction and competitive advantage.

In the end, however, the difficulties will be all the greater for companies that don't respond to this challenge in a timely fashion. One piece of evidence for this is the example of Korea, where Hyundai has worked hard for many years to build its reputation as the premier auto manufacturer to work for. Other manufacturing companies in Korea, as they try to attract talent, have a constant challenge finding, attracting, and retaining the best engineers. After all, if they're that good, they are, undoubtedly, already working for Hyundai.

3. NEW CUSTOMERS

Manufacturing leaders have seen their orders shoot up in recent years. Markets in Eastern Europe, East Asia, Latin America, and elsewhere around the world are growing rapidly. And despite the popularity of the "BRICs" acronym developed at Goldman Sachs (the idea that Brazil, Russia, India, and China are leading a new phase of global economic activity), many companies still underestimate the potential size of these markets, and the speed with which they are changing. There is an enormous unrecognized wave of demand that has just begun to appear and that will put many manufacturers in a catch-up game of backlogs and uncertain investment decisions around the world.

As they decide how to grow their businesses to meet this demand, industrial suppliers will struggle to satisfy all their customers. Consider, for example, the case of SCA Packaging, a unit of Sweden's Svenska Cellulosa Aktiebolaget. Out of the blue, one of its largest and most dependable customers (call it Company A) asked to purchase a large number of new products (cardboard boxes) each year for use in emerging markets. SCA, like many companies facing unexpected market growth, was caught flat-footed. Recent demand had increased exponentially for products to satisfy the growing consumer markets in developed and emerging nations. Consequently, the need for cartons in which to place these products had snowballed. SCA could not increase manufacturing capacity rapidly enough to meet Company A's order, at least not without cutting back on the supplies it had promised to other companies.

There was an added wrinkle: Company A, like many companies operating within the tight margins of emerging markets, was a tough price negotiator, and SCA had been earning a relatively small profit on its purchases. In short, if SCA attempted to satisfy Company A, it would lose business from customers that provided more profits on a per-box basis.

SCA's management applied computer simulations to look at this conundrum in more depth; they generated a detailed software-based model of the global business, its costs, and its revenues. The models included basic operations: the various cutting, printing, and gluing operations involved in producing the manufacturer's custom-made corrugated boxes. But they also included the events that many analyses leave out: the challenges and costs of managing (or failing to manage) demand and capacity warehouse usage and other value chain concerns. What, for instance, were the costs involved in avoiding "missed deliveries," or in dealing with unexpected processing line failures? In SCA's computerized depiction, the company's operations leaders could run simulated "experiments" and explore the likely consequences of different decisions without real risk.

The model quickly turned up a surprise. While Company A was seen as the primary cash-flow drain among major customers, the model revealed that serving "Company B," one of SCA's largest customers, was not as profitable as it appeared. Company B had always paid very high prices for boxes, but the irregularity of its ordering behavior created a hidden cost; it forced SCA to hold a large inventory. In fact, SCA dropped Company B and took on the new demands of Company A. In one factory alone, the packaging company's inventory costs fell by 30 percent, and profits rose by $200,000—all within a quarter. SCA is currently rolling the model out to its other factories (roughly 100 in total) and extending it to examine other supply chain and transportation issues as well.

The point is not to suggest that every manufacturer facing unprecedented global markets needs to start computer modeling. However, consider this: How many manufacturers would have reached the same decision that SCA reached? As the buildup of the global middle class continues (and it almost certainly will accelerate), how many similar dilemmas will emerge for other manufacturers? And what is the necessary learning curve for mastering those dilemmas—especially when the best decisions, as SCA discovered, are often not obvious?

To be sure, distinctive manufacturers have gotten used to following their customers around the world. But the speed of the current expansion is new. Emerging markets with huge product-hungry consumer bases in Brazil, the Middle East, Asia, and, more slowly, some African states are suddenly clamoring for a much higher volume of new and existing products served up locally.

The resulting dilemma is simple: This represents a tremendous opportunity for manufacturers, very few of which will be able to afford to remain isolated, serving only their current familiar markets. But most manufacturing industries have gradually built up their practices through decades of stable, incremental market growth. Many companies, keenly aware of the risks in entering new markets, are not prepared to react fast enough and well enough to make a place for themselves in this new environment. Few manufacturers have the capital, knowledge, or partnerships needed to accelerate their manufacturing operations effectively on that kind of global scale.

New markets also mean new types of competitors. The growth of local industrial entrepreneurship in Asia, Latin America, the Middle East, and Africa—often reinforced by governmental sponsorship and national pride—is leading to a host of local mainstream businesses, many of which will become multinational manufacturers in their own right. These companies are not bound by the old "brownfield" (long-established) industrial base of North American and European companies; as upstarts, they can leapfrog past outdated technology (which they typically do) and moribund practices (which they do far less often).

To respond effectively, established manufacturers are finding themselves forced to site their factories on a larger geographic scale. Making items in Western factories and shipping them to these distant ports is far too slow and uneconomical for many fast-paced, interconnected business environments with increasing delivery obligations. The alternative is a decentralized global/local strategy, in which manufacturers site more plants in more locations around the world, trying to build them so they can be easily dismantled *or* expanded as business conditions shift. But today, companies prepared for this strategy (e.g, companies with even the simplest enablers of transportability, such as modular and skid-mounted production equipment), are few and far between. So, to accomplish this, manufacturers have two formidable tasks. The first is to generate and manage the extra financial capital needed for flexible networks. The second is to develop the intellectual capital and sophisticated business intelligence needed to move factory operations quickly to where demand, local regulations, competition, and other factors—such as access to a supply base—are optimal.

4. EXPANDING VARIETY

From the ever-widening line of Lego character toys (like Bionicles), to the thousands of variations of parts and components that go into "BMWs" and other luxury cars, to the one-at-a-time production system at Dell Computer, manufacturers are reinventing their product portfolios to eliminate the threat of commoditization. By differentiating their products—even to the point of making individually customized versions of them—they hope to attract a growing group of customers who live in a consumer age characterized by the mantra, "I want what I want."

Indeed, during the next few decades product variety is likely to expand even more as mass customization—the ability to personalize mass-produced products—gains in popularity. This is happening even in once staid sectors like industrial parts and building construction. For example, Architectural Glazing Technologies (AGT) in Waterboro, Maine (Exhibit 2-6) offers custom skylights that consumers and glazers design over the Internet, choosing

EXHIBIT 2-6 AGT'S CUSTOM-FABRICATED SKYLIGHTS

Photo courtesy of Architectural Glazing Technologies

styles, colors, sizes, shapes, and ornamentation. These options are fed into a computer-aided design system that produces the finished items in AGT's factories. For AGT, the price of offering this degree of variety would once have been beyond consideration. But now it is less expensive than operating as a batch production house. The company no longer has to test to determine which skylights may be "popular," manufacturing hundreds of each unit regardless of there being advance orders, keeping dozens in inventory, and devoting resources to selling those that don't make a hit.

The demand for more product variation exists in part, of course, because some companies can provide it—and because a growing number of consumers around the world require it. People buying, say, a kitchen table in Curitiba, Stockholm, Durban, Milan, or Bangkok may have very different images in mind of how that table should look and feel. The more mature a country's market becomes, the more diverse and varied are the products that its customers seek.

BMW's leaders realized this very early and built the company around a dedication to the value of variety. Their catalog now contains 350 model versions, 175 interior equipment options, 500 extra equipment options, and 90 standard colors. Altogether this leads to a staggering 10^{17} possible combinations for just their 7 Series and 10^{32} combinations across all platforms. Clearly this level of personalized demand is part of BMW's value proposition; and an increasing number of all automakers' customers will demand greater customizability as well.

But demand is not the only factor pushing variation. The speed of product research and development continues to accelerate even in industries where product life cycles have been notoriously slow in years gone by. Think, for example, of a simple plastic plumbing tube. For decades upon decades, plumbers and contractors have installed only one type of tube with very little variation, whether for a drinking fountain or a heating system in a floor. But now this singular item is a hydra-headed product. Some tubes bend, while others keep a rigid shape. Some are lined internally with recycled composites; others, with aluminum. And they are manufactured and sold in black, white, gray, and yellow even if, once installed behind the walls, they are not likely to be seen again.

As manufacturers find response in the market to these kinds of small amenities, they are discovering that varia-

tion is probably the only alternative they have to commoditization. Conversely, while it appears that product
variety has produced financial rewards at some manufacturers—BMW, Dell, Lego, and AGT included—many companies have failed to meet the corporate performance
results that were expected from a more diverse product
portfolio. There is actually a universal principle at play
here: in factories in virtually all industries, product portfolio complexity tends to be the single most significant
cost driver. And while complexity has grown slowly but
steadily in the past, the operational capabilities needed to
control and contain the associated costs have typically not
grown accordingly, and few manufacturing leaders seem
to fully calculate the impact or reorganize to meet it. For
example, among automakers, only one in seven production lines can accommodate multiple platforms. That
shows how far an industry—even one said to be the front-
runner in the race for flexible manufacturing—has to go
before it can efficiently capture the value of variety.

Without a clear eye on the costs of customization,
manufacturers can let the number of products and product varieties increase for years without curtailing their
portfolios. Maybe the most critical decision makers, the
CEO and top team, are oriented toward the marketing and
promotion of products, without a feel for the operational
costs and difficulties (or much interest in hearing about
them). In some cases, the continued expansion of the
product line is perceived as a core part of the company's
identity. Such was the case at Lego in the early 2000s,
when a sustained set of financial blows forced the company's leaders to begin to think differently.

LEGO'S COMPLEXITY CONUNDRUM

On the surface, the Lego Group didn't look as if it was in trouble. The fourth largest toymaker in the world at the time (today it is fifth largest), the Lego Group sold €1 billion ($1.35 billion) worth of Lego toys in 2004. Even in the digital age, these toys maintained a surprisingly firm grip on the market and seemed to adapt well to changing tastes. The company's steady stream of new products routinely generated three-quarters of its yearly sales. Popular enthusiasm was so great that in 2000, the British Association of Toy Retailers joined *Fortune* magazine in naming the company's classic bricks "the toy of the century."

But the Lego Group's financial performance told another story. The Lego Group had lost money four out of the seven years from 1998 through 2004. Sales dropped 30 percent in 2003 and 10 percent more in 2004, when profit margins stood at 30 percent. Lego Group executives estimated that the company was destroying €250,000 ($337,000) in value every day.

How could such a seemingly successful toymaker lose that much money? A great part of it was due to the complexity of its product line. This was no small matter for the Lego Group, which, by the time CEO Jorgen Vig Knudstorp took the helm in 2004, had grown to roughly 7,300 employees, working mostly in two factories and three packaging centers—each in a different country—turning out more than 10,000 permutations of its products packaged in hundreds of configurations.

For example, the "Kitchen," the company's product development lab, was a point of corporate pride. But new products were delivering less and less profit. Each successive generation of offerings added more complexity. Plastic bricks and other elements that were once available only in primary colors, plus black and white, now came in more than 100 hues. A pirate kit included 8 pirates with 10 types of legs in different attire and positions.

Such intricacy and attention to detail reflected the firm's culture of craftsmanship, but also its disregard for the costs of innovation. The company designers were dreaming up new toys without fully factoring in the price of materials or the costs of production.

Furthermore, just 30 products generated 80 percent of sales, while two-thirds of the company's 1,500-plus stock-keeping units (SKUs) were items that it no longer manufactured. The Lego Group also dealt with an astonishing array of suppliers, more than 11,000 in all. That's nearly twice as many suppliers as Boeing uses to build its airplanes. The company ran one of the largest injection-molding operations in the world, with more than 800 machines, in its Danish factory, yet the production teams operated as hundreds of independent toy shops. The teams placed their orders haphazardly and changed them frequently, preventing operations from piecing together a reliable picture of demand needs, supply capabilities, and inventory levels. This murkiness led to overall capacity utilization of just 70 percent.

In such a fragmented system, long-term planning can be exceptionally difficult. Day-to-day operations were often chaotic. Operators routinely responded to last-minute demands, readily implementing costly changeovers. That the Lego Group's production sites were located in such high-cost countries as Denmark, Switzerland, and the United States put the company at a further disadvantage.

As part of a transformation overseen by CEO Knudstorp, starting in 2004, Lego began to address these concerns. Mads Nipper, the company's chief of product innovation, worked closely with Bali Padda, who oversees the supply chain, to devise a series of day-to-day solutions to the paradox of constraints. Nipper and Padda recommended slicing the palette of roughly 100 colors in half. They also recommended cutting back on the thousands of different police officers, pirates, and other figures in production. The team took a deliberate approach to analyzing the true costs of each element and identifying those elements whose costs were out of line with the rest of the stock. This initiative, coupled with a raw materials sourcing study, helped the Lego Group cut its resin costs in half and shrink its supplier roster by 80 percent.

At the same time, the operational team put a process in place to help designers make more cost-effective choices. Team members devised basic rules regarding the creation of new colors and shapes and spelled out the requirements for ordering new materials. They also created a cost matrix, clearly showing the price associated with each change. Once the costs of innovation were clear, designers were urged to use existing elements in new ways, rather than devise new elements requiring new molds and colors. The initiative encouraged the designers to think in terms of price trade-offs when they were developing a new item: Yes, you can give sparkling amber eyes to your new Bionicle space alien action figure, but it may limit your choices on its claws.

Cost transparency gave developers a new way to define their achievement. "The best cooks are not the ones who have all the ingredients in front of them. They're the ones who go into whatever kitchen and work with whatever they have," wrote a senior manager in a memo to the Lego Group's own Kitchen. The designers seemed to take those words to heart. The product development group "initially saw reducing complexity as pure pain," says Knudstorp, "but gradually they realized that what they had seen at first as a new set of constraints could in fact enable them to become even more creative."

—Keith Oliver, Edouard Samakh, and Peter Heckmann, "Rebuilding Lego, Brick by Brick," *strategy+business*, Autumn 2007.

This trend of increasing variation and complexity is also raising challenges for the makers of production machines. Can they develop more agile equipment that can produce a variety of different products, guarantee change-overs, improve throughput from start to finish of a product life cycle, and lower capital expenditures? Additionally, this new wave of machines will increasingly have to conform to global standards. Otherwise, it will not be feasible for manufacturers to transfer capacity around the world as demand fluctuates. Some production equipment makers have not yet gotten the message, but others have begun to recognize this shift and gear up for it.

5. ENVIRONMENTAL PRESSURE

It's not surprising that, in recent years, many corporations have publicly embraced environmentalism and the need to address the problem of global climate change. They fundamentally recognize that it is better to lead in improving the environment than to be pushed. In early 2007, CEOs and chairmen from 10 of the largest corporations in the United States—including General Electric, DuPont, Alcoa, BP America, Duke Energy, and Caterpillar—gathered with the heads of four major nonprofits to urge Congress to pass legislation that, among other things, would spur the growth of green technologies and create a mandatory "cap and trade" program limiting greenhouse gases. The group, U.S. Climate Action Partnership (USCAP), stressed that by proactively dealing with the issue, companies can earn a voice in planning policy and thus avoid "stroke of the pen" risks, in which new government rules can undermine a company's value overnight.

"If you're not at the table when these [climate-change-related] negotiations are going on," says James Rogers, Duke Energy's CEO, "you're going to be on the menu."

The world's manufacturing companies will shoulder much of the burden of reducing their own "carbon footprints": the amount of measurable CO_2 that they each emit into the atmosphere each year. As the cost of traditional forms of energy rises, and measures to control carbon and other pollutants are mandated by policymakers, manufacturers will have to find ways to minimize traditional energy use, develop renewable energy sources and grids, protect local water supplies, and meet stricter regulatory reporting requirements. In all, industry is responsible for 15 to 20 percent of greenhouse emissions in the world. Manufacturing companies that neglect this issue may see their performance gains undone by energy cost increases. Those that embrace environmental quality may see their products become more acceptable, and they may meet future regulations more efficiently.

At the same time, smart companies are identifying business opportunities that go beyond carbon footprint reduction, and connecting greenhouse gas reduction to core business strategies. Alcoa has pledged that 50 percent of its products will come from recycled aluminum by 2020—a significant cost-saving move, because recycled aluminum requires a fraction of the energy required to produce primary aluminum. Airbus, the European airplane manufacturer, has stated that it will cut CO_2 emissions from its planes by 50 percent before 2020, and nitrous oxide emissions by 80 percent. This in itself is a stunningly bold objective; for example, it could require a doubling of fuel efficiency over that time period. Achieving the goal will require a cross-industry effort by Airbus and its Tier 1 suppliers; it will also require a range of entirely new products.

DuPont, meanwhile, has made fundamental shifts away from businesses that are heavily reliant on fossil fuels by selling its Dacron and Nylon divisions and focusing on high-growth businesses making biobased materials. This change is evidenced by DuPont's acquisition of Pioneer Hi-Bred International, a seed company specializing in biotechnology and genetic engineering.

DuPont has been particularly aggressive in setting high environmental targets. For example, the manufacturer expects the output of its titanium technologies division to double between 1990 and 2010, but its energy use is slated to increase by only 40 percent—a serious constraint, because energy constitutes a significant percentage of the selling price of titanium dioxide. Other, less energy-intensive units will have even higher benchmarks. So far, the titanium technologies unit is achieving its aim. "Inspirational goals call an organization to act beyond conventional boundaries," says Craig Heinrich, leader of DuPont's global energy team for titanium technologies. "An easy goal fails to challenge the creative potential of the organization."

Exhibit 2-7 gives some cost estimates, developed for the European Union, for carbon reduction measures that might be taken by different types of manufacturers.

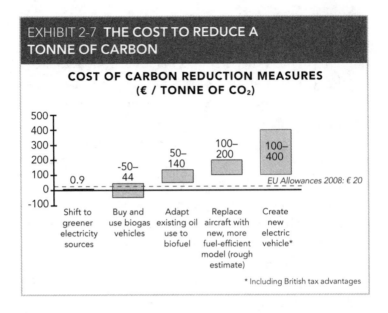

EXHIBIT 2-7 **THE COST TO REDUCE A TONNE OF CARBON**

COST OF CARBON REDUCTION MEASURES
(€ / TONNE OF CO₂)

For manufacturers, one of the obvious places to start reducing emissions is the supply chain, especially in a high-energy-use, distributed network where there are always opportunities for improvement. Often, the kind of thinking required to reduce emissions is the same kind of thinking that can reduce all sorts of waste and inefficiency in a production process.

For example: In 2006, the Carbon Trust, a United Kingdom–based research and advisory group, discovered a "perverse incentive" in the sourcing of raw potatoes for manufacturing snack foods like potato chips. Because prices for potatoes are set by weight, farmers typically control humidification to produce a moister and therefore heavier vegetable. Even within the strictly limited specifications of moisture content set by the food manufacturers, these few grams of extra water are significant. In the chip-manufacturing process, the additional cooking needed to burn them off accounted for an unexpectedly high percentage of the chips' energy consumption and carbon output.

The recommended solution, as the Carbon Trust put it, was to change the procurement contract: to provide farmers with an incentive to produce potatoes with less moisture. This would better position the manufacturers to take advantage of carbon trading credits and other regulations for greenhouse gas reduction. And it would set a precedent for further collaboration between food makers and their agricultural suppliers.

As the work of the Carbon Trust shows, the impact of continuous improvement methods in this field is enormous. But environmental challenges are also more complex than people realize at first glance.

The difficulties have less to do with the technologies, or the carbon reduction methods, and more to do with the establishment of relationships. The manufacturing team may not be focused on establishing connections with the outside world; those connections are typically established by marketing and community relations groups. But environmental pressures are bringing the two traditionally discrete functions of manufacturing and public affairs together. This phenomenon increasingly will put manufacturers on the spot, especially in developing countries like Mexico, Brazil, India, China, and Thailand as they go through their next stages of market and regulatory evolution.

For example, as a harbinger of the types of regulations that may become routine in the future, eight Indian states have imposed full or partial bans on the sale and production of Coca Cola and Pepsi based on environment-related allegations. Both companies are vigorously defending themselves, but no matter what the eventual outcome, the stakes are particularly high: Coke and Pepsi share a nearly $1.5 billion market in India, which is one of the fastest-growing soft drink consumer regions in the world.

The regulatory challenge in manufacturing will affect corporations and governments alike. They will have to sift through competing claims and make judgments about the risks of products and processes. And since risk, by its nature, is ambiguous because chemicals and other emissions affect different people differently, and since health and environmental effects often take years to appear, the causal chain almost always will be ambiguous. Corporations will have to figure out how best to change their practices in the light of that ambiguity.

So far, in the 200-year history of manufacturing production, there has been a relatively high level of trust established between manufacturers and society in general. Very few manufactured products have led to such high levels of environmental and health damage that they had to be banned or recalled. But one never knows when the next crisis will occur. For instance, what impact will the 2007 recall of almost a million preschool toys made with lead paint—the first recall in its history for the highly quality-conscious toy manufacturer Fisher Price (owned by Mattel)—have on the Chinese role as a production supplier of inexpensive toys to the United States? In this case, the recall led directly to an agreement between the Chinese and American governments to prohibit the release of any of the lead-sealed toys. (The specific agencies making the agreement were the U.S. Consumer Products Safety Council and the Chinese General Administration of Quality Supervision, Inspection and Quarantine.) If the Chinese are unable to enforce the ban, the issue will probably re-emerge.

THE CASE OF MATERIALS POOLING: MEETING THE ENVIRONMENTAL CHALLENGE

Starting in 2002, a particularly passionate consortium, known as the Materials Pooling Project, demonstrated exactly how difficult—and valuable—it will be to face the environmental challenge head on in manufacturing.

Some members of the consortium are household-name companies: Nike, Ford, BP, Unilever, Harley-Davidson, Hewlett-Packard. Others are specialized, innovative manufacturers with an environmental identity: Aveda (a division of Estée Lauder dedicated to ecological cosmetics) and Plug Power (a pioneering fuel cell company). The consortium also includes Sikorsky (a helicopter manufacturer), Pratt & Whitney (the jet engine division of United Technologies Corporation), and, at various times, about 20 component and commodity suppliers, of which the largest and most consistently present is Visteon, a former division of Ford. They come together under the joint auspices of the Rocky Mountain Institute (RMI), a well-known think tank led by energy-efficiency and "hypercar"expert Amory Lovins, and the Society for Organizational Learning (SoL), an international group focused on organizational learning practice, founded by *Fifth Discipline* author Peter Senge.

The consortium was set up for manufacturers to pool their purchasing power to favor raw materials that are freer of toxins and waste, and easier to recycle or reuse; this gives suppliers more of an incentive to provide such materials. It was founded by Michael Braungart, the coauthor, with architect William McDonough, of an unusual and influential book called *Cradle to Cradle: Remaking the Way We Make Things* (North Point Press, 2002). The book points out that nearly every mass-produced product, from chair fabrics to children's toys to printer cartridges, contains trace elements of heavy metals and mutagenic materials. In aggregate, over time, these might be hidden causes of cancer, infertility, and genetic damage (although it is difficult to know for certain).

Mr. Braungart proposed the idea of a materials pooling subgroup to the Society of Organizational Learning, which has a large number of corporate members. And indeed the idea proved popular with member companies, who felt their license to operate depended, more than ever before, on meeting and transcending environmental regulations. Automakers, for example, faced a pending European Union rule called the "End-of-Life Vehicle Directive," with such targets as 85 percent automobile recyclability by weight by 2006, and 95 percent by 2015. (If you count scrap metal, 75 percent of the material in most cars is already recycled.) "The directives had us thinking," recalls Visteon's Matt Roman. "If we were to take back and recycle our components whenever a car was scrapped, what would that framework look like?"

Pressure also came from increased liabilities and regulations concerning product toxicity. Consider, for example, hexavalent chromium, which is routinely used in engine parts and fasteners. It's inexpensive, prevents corrosion, resists wear, and shines appealingly even when scratched. But when swallowed or inhaled, it is highly carcinogenic. (The crime that triggers the lawsuit in Steven Soderbergh's film *Erin Brockovich* is carelessness with hexavalent chromium.) New European regulations have outlawed its use in automobiles since 2006, and manufacturers of other products recognize the public affairs benefit and general moral benefit of reducing this material. At Harley-Davidson, Hugh Vallely, the director of motorcycle product planning until his retirement in 2004, raised the point simply: "If this material is so toxic, why are we using it?"

By mid-2003, there were four active groups of companies in the Materials Pooling Project, focusing respectively on replacing hexavalent chromium; sourcing lightweight corrugated cardboard; researching the environmental impact of different types of leather (as used in Nike shoes and Visteon seats); and managing polypropylene, a plastic resin often used in consumer packaging. There was a constant swirl of activity: weekly phone calls to each group and quarterly project meetings of unusual enthusiasm. "We were on the leading edge of a field that was just starting to take off," says Aveda's vice president of package development, John Delfausse. "Not only did we really want to be there, but light bulbs started turning on. 'We could do this.'" They talked about rethinking product design in Braungartian fashion. They also found unexpected connections—Mr. Delfausse, for example, recalls scoring a potential cache of recycled polypropylene, to be used in lipstick caps, from an electronics supplier who shipped disk drives in plastic racks. "I've got tons of this stuff, and we would love to harvest it for you," the supplier said.

But by 2004, two years after the project was founded, momentum had slowed and goals were scaled back. One fundamental roadblock was the differences among the companies themselves. This showed up most dramatically in the group working on hexavalent chromium. Pratt & Whitney and Sikorsky needed functionality; stainless steel was potentially acceptable. But Harley-Davidson needed beautiful, rust-resistant chrome for the kind of visible engine components that could endure exposure to a beach full of salt spray and emerge gleaming in the sun. If they couldn't keep hexavalent, they'd have to find another kind of chrome. And Ford was part of the USCAR consortium, which announced a decision to switch to trivalent chromium, a material approved by European regulations. All these differences eroded the group's potential collective purchasing clout.

Getting cooperation from suppliers was also unexpectedly difficult. Having agreed to canvass their suppliers for details about materials, many of the corporate members returned empty-handed. Some suppliers apparently suspected that this was just another tactic to squeeze down prices. Other suppliers had never kept track of their materials' environmental pedigree—the detailed history of their previous uses (if they were recycled), their contact with contaminants, or their exact chemical makeup. And then suppliers had their own constraints; John Delfausse's electronics supplier, for example, discovered that it did not have the contractual right to pass on the polypropylene to Aveda.

Consortium members talked openly about all these issues, but there was another, more hidden factor limiting the growth of the consortium: the discomfort members felt about sharing information with competitors. Suppliers were also skittish about competition, which put the whole project in a sort of catch-22, because participating companies feared they could be vulnerable to U.S. antitrust charges if no competing suppliers were present, but they were unable to compel competing suppliers to join.

Underlying these concerns was a more visceral issue. It's hard enough to talk openly with people from other industries about the differences, say, between shoe leather and car-seat leather; to eliminate all potential toxins from materials would require almost unimaginable openness. Manufacturers and suppliers alike would have to entrust competitors with some of their most carefully held secrets.

The Materials Pooling Project companies are still working through these issues, one component at a time. And in a world where energy and materials technology breakthroughs are seemingly on the horizon, their experience provides a useful way to learn to deal with the next round of challenges. As engineers engage in unprecedented forms of collaboration across organizational boundaries, will they ultimately make their companies stronger? Or weaker? Although initiatives like the Materials Pooling Project show how difficult these questions are to answer, they also show how important it will be to answer them well.

—Art Kleiner, "Materials Witnesses,"
strategy + business, Spring 2005

The burgeoning need for more environmentally friendly production processes will naturally translate to additional stress on the process innovation efforts in virtually all industries. Newly designed manufacturing equipment will likely have to be able to process new materials; materials in short supply will have to be replaced; all of this will have to happen in ways that are flexible enough to cover the growing demand for customization and at the same time consume less energy, using inputs that are less prone to cause environmental damage.

6. NEW COMPETITION

Just a few years ago, after decades of consolidation, it seemed in many industries that two or three companies had virtual control of many product categories. The barriers of entry were perceived as just too high to overcome, and few large companies were interested in entering new mature consumer products or automobile categories.

That has changed. One can no longer assume that a given industry sector is "sewn up," not even in the company's home territory. Some of the most successful manufacturers on the global scene in the past year or two have come seemingly from out of nowhere and are bursting on the scene as their predecessors from Korea and Japan did, and before that their nineteenth-century predecessors in the United States and Europe. Noteworthy new global manufacturing competitors include Haier, the Chinese appliance maker; Tata Sons and its many subsidiaries in India (and now, increasingly, elsewhere); Mexico's Gruma, a producer of food-related technologies (such as flatbread makers); Gerdau Ameristeel, a minimill steel producer with roots in Brazil, Canada, Germany, and the United States; and SABMiller, the South Africa–based brewery.

The changing mix of global competition has led to heightened competition for multinationals, as well as for the local companies that used to enjoy relatively clear playing fields. Further, the pace at which the mix is changing is accelerating to match the speed at which investment capital moves to more advantageous locales and creates new major players.

GRUMA: A NEW TYPE OF GLOBAL COMPETITOR

Gruma SA, a company headquartered near Monterrey, Mexico, is the sort of enterprise that you might expect to operate solely within its country's borders. Its main line of business in Mexico is the production of corn flour and related products, highly sought-after commodities in a land where corn is plentiful and tortillas are a staple. But Gruma is also a $2.5 billion international powerhouse with manufacturing plants in the United States, Venezuela, Costa Rica, the United Kingdom, and China.

Gruma's Shanghai facility is enormous. At the time of its opening in October 2006, it represented a $100 million investment; and could annually produce 15,000 tons of wheat tortillas, 7,000 tons of corn tortillas, and 6,000 tons of snacks. It found ready customers among Asian distributors in Japan, Korea, Singapore, Hong Kong, Thailand, the Philippines, and Taiwan. And Gruma immediately began sizing up new markets just over the horizon. "In the first stage, we will supply the continental China market, gradually increasing our range to the European and Asian borders of the Middle East. To us, this is a long-term investment that will lead to strategic new business opportunities," says Roberto Gonzalez Barrera, chairman of Gruma.

—Alfonso Martinez and Ronald Haddock, "The Flatbread Factor," *strategy+business*, Spring 2007

The building products sector is a good example. By now, the emergence of Chinese manufacturing in this sector is well established. And this is not limited to the relocation of individual factories to China, still operated by companies in the United States. American companies have also outsourced their operations to Chinese manufacturers entirely—and educated those suppliers to improve their quality and productivity.

In building products, as in many other industries, the growth of private-label alternatives, which typically feature lower costs and create price pressure on established brands, have also created new competition. For example, many of the major plumbing product distributors have launched high-quality, private-label brands, and Home Depot, the large home improvement chain, has also launched and licensed many private-label products which it sources directly from Chinese producers.

Taken together, the outsourcing of operations and the demand for private labels have supported the emergence of many new producers in China. As many as 100 new competitors, with the ability to produce to any standard, have sprung up in various sectors of the building products industry. In fact, because many of these new competitors lack distribution channels in Western markets, there is considerable interest in buying weaker U.S. companies to get direct access to this market. Given the cash available in Asia and from Western private equity, this very quickly could create even more fundamental shifts in the industry.

The emergence of new competitors is having a significant impact on the automotive supply industry, too. The major car makers in the United States have found that sourcing directly from local Asian suppliers represents a lower-cost, albeit a riskier, solution than using their existing suppliers' Asian factories to meet demand. The local suppliers are less expensive because they usually do not have a high overhead structure to support, and they are less affected by established oligopolies. This is one reason why there is so much impetus within the U.S. automotive supply base to move overhead and engineering activities to China and India.

The effort and risk involved in developing these local suppliers can be daunting, but that has not slowed the drive to capture the cost savings. Even Japanese car makers, who generally support their best suppliers as opposed to squeezing them for lower prices, are very interested in the emerging supply base. So are European automakers. Indeed, many Japanese and European companies have already signed supply contracts with local Chinese producers.

New competitors in almost every industry will make life for established Western manufacturers more difficult, and typically, the manufacturing function will bear the brunt in the form of performance pressure. In addition to the effects of direct competition from new companies, there is an indirect microeconomic effect, too. The prospect of growing markets, especially in Asia, combined with the entry of ambitious new competitors appears to be upsetting cyclical patterns in manufacturing capacity.

In China, for example, the urgency to establish capacity is perceived as so high that hasty decisions are being made that do not necessarily account for all the factors involved (including the presence of other new competitors). "Let's put in another square kilometer now," the reasoning goes, "because it is easier than having to plan additional facilities in a few years. And anyway, if we end up with overcapacity in China, we'll just close plants in Europe or the United States."

There are times when that type of logic makes sense, but there are also times when one should, at the very least, hedge one's bets. Take the current vehicle production capacity in China. At 8 million units, it has already well exceeded the expected sales of 5.5 million vehicles in 2007. By 2010, it is expected to reach 20 million units, far outpacing anticipated sales of only 9 million vehicles. Yet, automakers such as Volkswagen , General Motors, and Toyota are spending some $15 billion to boost annual capacity in China, further compounding fears of an impending glut.

Some believe that these new competitors with global ambitions can be stopped by moving over time to a less liberal, less open trade regime. Thus, in 2007, newly elected French President Nicolas Sarkozy vowed to protect his nation's industrial base by restricting trade agreements and installing takeover controls; the United States was increasingly aggressive in its demand that China create a more level manufacturing landscape (for instance, by revaluing the yuan); and several groups in the United States were calling for more product safeguards for imports, or even for limiting certain product categories that could be imported (e.g., for the sake of safety).

But no matter how it is dealt with, the presence of new competitors is a challenge for everyone. And there are no obvious rules when so many companies are coming from so many different backgrounds to make products for the same customers. Sometimes, the home company has an advantage—but not always. Sometimes, the race goes to the most innovative, and sometimes to the most stable.

The important questions are how to react now and how to identify new threats as they arise. The most successful companies see threats while their peers remain unaware of them or unfocused on them. The best companies react with thoughtful, timely decision making while the rest struggle along until only complete restructuring will save them. The best companies see potential threats and opportunities and set their own future direction in advance. The rest are frozen out—unable to make major decisions about investments, footprints, and improvement efforts because they do not think strategically. These companies should beware of a new competitor from some unexpected place thinking strategically about them.

7. LABOR CONFLICT

Strikes and walkouts are not a thing of the past. Between 1984 and 2004, there were more strikes in Western European companies than occurred between 1955 and 1975. But strikes are not the cause of labor conflict; they are only one symptom. The real cause is the difficult history of labor relations in most factories and manufacturing companies over the past century. Plants that *haven't* suffered strikes are often just as problematic as plants that have; their workforces have simply found different ways to complain.

In most plants, treatment of the workforce and management attitudes toward labor are reminiscent of the nineteenth century. And most manufacturers are at a loss for ways to improve their engagement with plant workers. This can be illustrated by the success rates of programs that are in part implemented to motivate the workforce

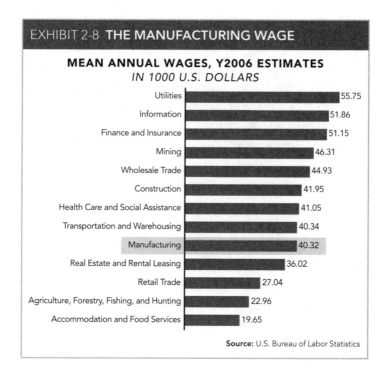

EXHIBIT 2-8 **THE MANUFACTURING WAGE**

MEAN ANNUAL WAGES, Y2006 ESTIMATES
IN 1000 U.S. DOLLARS

Utilities	55.75
Information	51.86
Finance and Insurance	51.15
Mining	46.31
Wholesale Trade	44.93
Construction	41.95
Health Care and Social Assistance	41.05
Transportation and Warehousing	40.34
Manufacturing	40.32
Real Estate and Rental Leasing	36.02
Retail Trade	27.04
Agriculture, Forestry, Fishing, and Hunting	22.96
Accommodation and Food Services	19.65

Source: U.S. Bureau of Labor Statistics

with sweeping bottom-up reforms. Programs in total quality management, Six Sigma, and other forms of continuous improvement are more often than not disappointing.

One major driver of motivation in shop floor environments is compensation (fear and pride are the other two). So one can begin to understand why manufacturing has lost its cachet as a career by comparing its wages with other sectors of employment. In 2006, for instance, mean annual wages in manufacturing were significantly lower than those in the health care, transportation, construction, and mining sectors (see Exhibit 2-8).

Moreover, few corporate leaders have made strides in aligning factory workers closely to the companies that employ them. Only 20 percent of production workers in Western Europe and the United States receive compensation that is linked to performance in any way, and more than 75 percent work within a salary system so rigid that it drives people to take overtime (although that is rarely the intent of the system).

As conditions fail to improve, morale levels among manufacturing workers are falling. In some older industrial nations, there is growing evidence of on-the-job worker depression. In France, for example, between November 2006 and November 2007, four workers killed themselves at the Renault Technocentre, an ultramodern automobile design facility in Guyancourt, near Paris. In notes and messages left behind—one taped to the Technocentre's door and another visible on the computer screen at a victim's empty desk—the men said that harsh conditions and extreme pressure on the job had made their lives unbearable.

During that same period three men took their lives at a French Peugeot plant, bitterly complaining about their jobs. And at least one other worker committed suicide at a manufacturing plant operated by the French power company EDF. These tragic events are new in France and have led to a great deal of press attention, leading to a public debate over whether such suicides ought to be qualified as work-related incidents or private incidents at an "unfortunate" location.

At best, events like these are signs of a dispiriting and unproductive human capital milieu in manufacturing. But few companies seem interested in improving things. Even fewer are known as showcases for good working conditions. Among the few that are regularly cited as manufac-

turing employers of choice are Semco, in Brazil; the Springfield Remanufacturing Group, in Springfield, Missouri;
and W. L. Gore and Associates, in Newark, Delaware. But if
more companies do not join their ranks—especially as
generation Y, which is accustomed to the free-form collo-
quy and relatively high levels of connectedness, enters the
workforce—manufacturing plants will soon seem more
depressing than ever.

With fewer workers to choose from in coming years,
the quality and capabilities of existing workers will become ever more critical. Workers will be asked to continually improve their productivity, deliver consistent quality
amid tighter and tighter lead times, and participate more
in corporate initiatives for quality or innovation. As a result, the role and impact of labor unions and other worker
advocacy groups, despite their relative impotence at present, will likely expand in the future. Further, any perception among workers that they have no voice or are not
appreciated could easily ignite ever greater industrial conflicts.

Some companies have sought to escape all this by moving their operations to low-wage countries—not just China
and India but Eastern Europe and elsewhere. They appear
to believe that moving to nations with poorer populations
that welcome even low wages means that they can afford to
disregard issues of social strife, quality, worker training,
and hence productivity and efficiency. But this is probably
a mistake.

To understand why, look no further than Mexico. Within
the space of several years, Mexico went from being the place
to manufacture to serve the U.S. market to being in close
competition with China for every manufacturing location

decision. There are many reasons for this shift in status, but one of the most prominent was mismanagement of the workforce.

U.S. companies, in particular, went into Mexico without looking for ways to upgrade the workforce and root out possible inefficiencies. Untrained middle managers were kept in place, overseeing outmoded plants. Many of the principles of lean manufacturing, including the engagement of the entire workforce, were ignored. Thus, the workforce in many of these Mexican plants remained extremely disconnected, and its overall productivity lagged its potential. This effect was even more exaggerated by the social dislocation caused by *maquiladora* plants located near the U.S. border, which drew upon a labor pool that generally left families behind for jobs, and, therefore, had little or no connection to the location or the employer. As these plants sought to keep their skilled workers, wages crept up from $3 to $5/hour in many plants, higher than the wages of the local economy, and much higher than the $1 to $2 per hour paid in China. Mexico quickly became uncompetitive on a pure cost basis, and with no skill, productivity, or technological advantages to compensate, its status as a manufacturing haven declined.

In the end, manufacturers may find that their ability to develop skilled and motivated human capital is their single greatest competitive advantage, regardless of where the manufacturing takes place. Far more important than the question, "Should we tolerate a union?" is the question, "How can we set up the workforce to help drive the improvements that make or break the company?"

Toyota represents a fascinating example of how this latter question can be answered. Its noteworthy focus on plant workers as a major source of innovation and continuous improvement has been a huge factor in its success. This is based not just on skills but on a philosophy and culture that positions problem solving as a core element in everyone's jobs. Toyota's production systems rely on two tenets that sometimes seem at odds with Western culture: rigorous standardization and continuous improvement at every level. Those of us with a military background from the past think of standardized work as the opposite of innovation. But Toyota's approach says you cannot improve unless you first have a set starting point, and then observe what needs to be improved.

The focus on improvement at every level and by every employee in such a system is impressive. For example, much of Toyota's system for presenting parts at each stage of the final assembly lines has been developed and honed by the assembly workers and their supervisors. Similarly, homemade automatic guided vehicles (AGVs) can be seen in several Toyota plants; these were crafted out of cheap parts by local shop floor people. Toyota typically does not buy the much more expensive high-tech AGVs.

While some American and European companies are inclined to adopt and sustain some critical practices from their Japanese competitors such as Toyota and Honda, the ability to create a continuous improvement culture at every level has been elusive, and this keeps them one step behind. Meanwhile, Toyota, with a great deal of effort, has had considerable success exporting its processes to its U.S. and European facilities. And it continues to attract a very high level of talent into skilled positions; people know now that simply working for Toyota will increase their "resale value" for being hired elsewhere, because of the company's policies, high pay (relative to the local markets), and reputation.

Moreover, even after all this success, Toyota's efforts around its manufacturing people have greatly accelerated in the last few years. The company continues to upgrade its global training centers, where thousands of workers, supervisors, and managers learn the underlying philosophy as well as the craft skills. These centers represent an unparalleled education effort that reaches all levels of the organization and focuses on manufacturing, in particular. Toyota has also "doubled down" by bolstering its employment screening processes to ensure that it hires people who, in addition to having basic skill levels, can learn the Toyota way. Finally, in many facilities, the company has assigned direct process ownership to hourly employees, so that improvement remains the responsibility of each individual.

In the end, Toyota's manufacturing workers feel that they are being invested in and that they are important. And, even though the pace of work at Toyota can be fast (as wasted effort continues to be reduced), unionization efforts in Georgetown and other facilities in the United States and Canada have so far fallen short. No one expects this to change anytime soon because Toyota keeps its workforce engaged and motivated— a competitive advantage in and of itself.

In general (examples such as Toyota notwithstanding), labor relations in manufacturing will engender more conflict in the future than in the past. While unions may not be the preferred communication mechanism everywhere, factory labor communities will have more and more bargaining power. After all, manufacturing employers will increasingly rely on higher skilled labor to handle the lean systems and new production technologies needed to master future challenges, *and* they also will find it increasingly difficult to attract and maintain employees because of demographic and socioeconomic factors. Factory workers will seize their newfound bargaining power, applying ever more sophisticated mechanisms of influence, such as cooperating with workers across borders to put pressure on employers by slowing critical links in the production chain.

8. MANAGEMENT CONFLICT

The final challenge is the troubled relationship that many manufacturing executives have with their own bosses and corporate leaders. In their seminal manufacturing management textbook, *Factory Physics,* Wallace Hopp and Mark Spearman decry the lack of influence that manufacturing executives have in most organizations. "America's manufacturing future," they wrote, "cannot help but be influenced by its past." Among other things, according to Hopp and Spearman, this past includes a "love affair" with finance and marketing that causes company leaders to overlook manufacturing and shows no sign of abating.

Many of the same conditions exist in Europe, where the status of manufacturing has long been subordinated to other corporate activities. Hence it is not surprising that CEOs—even of hard-core manufacturing companies—rarely have factory management backgrounds. Indeed, it is telling that between 1995 and 2005 in a targeted management publication like the *Harvard Business Review*, only 4 percent of the articles covered manufacturing and the supply chain; by contrast, between 1985 and 1995, 14 percent of the articles addressed these topics.

When financial or competitive pressures lead to cost cutting, manufacturing can be more affected than other functions. In a 2004 Booz Allen study of corporate transformation programs, which generally are initiated in highly competitive industries, manufacturing almost always had to pledge to produce the highest savings percentages. In fact, manufacturing (along with the procurement and purchasing functions) typically is expected to contribute a percentage of total expected savings that is much higher than its relative share of the cost base. Yet when competition relaxes, manufacturing rarely is given the opportunity to spend more freely again or replace lost capabilities. In short, manufacturing typically is a "cost savings cash cow"—an activity that, unlike marketing, sales, or customer service, is mostly hidden from consumers and, hence, is always a perfect candidate for reaping another 5 percent or 10 percent in spending cuts when the fear of competition drives a company to shore up profit margins. There are two problems with such financially driven top-down spending cuts: they often cut out potentially useful value-added activities, and they often fail to identify activities that *should* be cut out but aren't.

The lack of respect for manufacturing is driven partly by perception. Manufacturing is viewed typically as a less than critical function in a company, unless something goes wrong with the factories or supply chain. Also, manufacturing is not considered particularly connected to the bottom line, because investments in it tend to take an extraordinarily long time to come to fruition. For these reasons, the strategic emphasis at most corporations is directed toward product R&D, international expansion, brand acquisition, new enterprise resource planning, or ERP systems—in other words, anything but manufacturing.

PUTTING IT ALL TOGETHER

The eight primary challenges that manufacturing leaders must learn to navigate are very real, and in combination can have dire consequences if ignored. All of these challenges will require significantly more time from manufacturing leaders at all levels. They may also require more funds.

If these challenges are not addressed, the consequences could weaken the perceived ability of manufacturing to add value to the entire organization. Further, the success and failure of the manufacturing function is inextricably linked to the performance of the overall enterprise. In this sense, it's possible that these challenges will have the unintended result of making manufacturing more of a priority on the corporate agenda. But it may be too late for many companies: after years of neglect, their manufacturing capabilities may be too weak to cope with the dangerous mix of challenges that are gathering—either apparent now or ready to appear, perhaps as soon as the next shift begins.

ANTICIPATING MANUFACTURING CHALLENGES: AN ANALYTIC MODEL

Sometimes you can see the ramifications of a manufacturing choice in a simulated model, without having to actually suffer the consequences in the real world. Consider, for example, the case of HealthCo, a Western European pharmaceutical company with roughly $10 billion in annual revenue. HealthCo is at a "make or break" crossroads. Some executives hold the attitude that their manufacturing approach is just fine as is; why fix it if it isn't broken? Others advocate a more strategic role for manufacturing.

The challenges facing the company have brought this decision to a head. Like all pharmaceutical companies, it will face increasing pricing pressures from drug makers in countries where costs are low and generics producers are in evidence. The need for variety is also beginning to affect the industry; in the long term, as medicines are tailored to an individual patient's metabolism, size, physical condition, and genetic makeup, mass customization may be required. Further customization requirements could add immense complexity and cost to the manufacturing process. Meanwhile, as populations age in the West and fast-growing Asian markets develop, the demand for pharmaceuticals is quickly rising. And HealthCo is ill prepared. Pharmaceutical manufacturing processes require both technology-driven chemical and formulation lines and labor-intensive packaging lines, and HealthCo's aging network of

Western factories is neither sufficiently scaled nor innovative enough to operate efficiently. The investment capital to upgrade is not easily available either.

What should HealthCo do? In our model, built with HealthCo's representatives, we ran two scenarios. In each, we incorporated the same eight challenges facing manufacturing. The difference between the scenarios was HealthCo's approach to manufacturing. In Scenario 1, manufacturing was treated as usual, namely, in an opportunistic, short-term fashion. In Scenario 2, manufacturing received higher status (and funding) and more freedom to operate from a long-term perspective.

1. Some characteristics of Scenario 1 ("Business as Usual") include

  ➤ The leaders of the company decide not to adopt lean systems or change manufacturing in any other significant way. Instead, during a company-wide restructuring, HealthCo earmarks €2 million for a three-year, partial lean implementation—a minimal commitment in which the company focuses only on quick hit cost reductions, such as layoffs in its galenic production, packaging plants, or general site infrastructure. As a result, the company achieves a 3 percent annual productivity improvement but no lasting transformation.

  ➤ The company's approach to product variety continues to be unstructured and undisciplined; it simply adds new product lines one at a time and uses off-the shelf equipment to satisfy production needs. Complexity rises and the number of batch production changeovers explodes. Annual complexity costs quickly increase 5 percent. Meanwhile, to meet growing global demand, HealthCo adds significant new manufacturing capacity to its existing brownfield plants between 2011 and 2013. But in expanding its existing sites, the company's cost structure remains virtually the same.

2. Some characteristics of Scenario 2 ("Proactive Change") include

➤ HealthCo's management understands that if lean processes are to enhance operations, patience is necessary; small gains have to be measured and built upon to eventually reap large rewards. They invest about €5 million annually, from 2008 until 2020, in a lean transformation program. The upshot: HealthCo achieves a consistent 8 percent annual productivity improvement from 2010 onward, as its investment begins to pay off.

➤ Led by the chief manufacturing officer, the company takes a structured approach to reducing in-plant complexity and avoiding significant cost increases. HealthCo installs flexible production equipment capable of rapid product changeovers. It uses dedicated high-capacity chemical reaction units for high-volume products and smaller reactors for small-batch production. In addition, the company adapts its product design efforts and supply chain. It creates common designs in the early stages of production and in packaging layouts, thereby keeping the need for different materials to the absolute minimum. With all these measures in place, the company's annual complexity costs rise by only a couple of percentage points.

➤ To meet demand growth, the company seizes the opportunity to invest in new greenfield sites in the West and in Asia. These feature built-in lean principles and the flexibility to customize drugs and packaging. The company reduces its cost structure by 15 percent.

The model shows the financial implications of both approaches (see Exhibit 2-9). Business as Usual tactics produce a better cash flow initially—between 2007 and 2009. But in the long term, it would cause a cash-flow gap that would cripple the company and render it uncompetitive. By 2015, HealthCo's financial health would be irreversibly damaged. Looking at a longer time horizon that stretches out to 2020, the proactive approach creates a much greater return. In fact, when we model the company's performance, we find that the proactive approach creates €170 million (34 percent of 2007 EBIT) in additional shareholder value (net present value of the increase in cash flow).

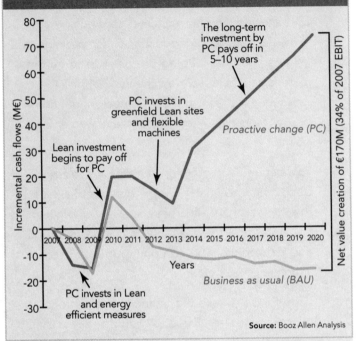

EXHIBIT 2-9 **MAKE OR BREAK MODELED FOR A PHARMACEUTICAL COMPANY**

The long-term investment by PC pays off in 5–10 years

PC invests in greenfield Lean sites and flexible machines

Lean investment begins to pay off for PC

Proactive change (PC)

Incremental cash flows (M€)

Net value creation of €170M (34% of 2007 EBIT)

Years

Business as usual (BAU)

PC invests in Lean and energy efficient measures

Source: Booz Allen Analysis

This analysis raises an essential question: why do companies respond differently to similar manufacturing challenges? The answer generally lies in the status that senior management affords manufacturing and its role in the company's performance.

Too often, companies give up on manufacturing and make shortsighted decisions, such as cutting back on plant investments, neglecting the value of lean tools, or outsourcing strategic production. Over long periods of time, this approach consistently produces dismal results compared to those of more enlightened competitors. Manufacturing-engaged senior management—predisposed to take a proactive view—ensures that manufacturing is front and center in company strategy and is ultimately rewarded as the challenges faced by manufacturing become more complex and intractable.

For notes and resources visit our Web site:
www.businessfuture.com

3

VIRTUOUS AND VICIOUS CYCLES

CAN A NATIONAL industry develop virtually overnight? Obviously, it can: look at the dramatic rise of manufacturing in China and the Middle East. Can a company that is seemingly invulnerable to competition suddenly collapse from manufacturing weaknesses? Here, too, the answer is yes. Many formerly thriving manufacturers can confirm this from their own experience.

But events like these are often misinterpreted. Many corporate collapses, for instance, are not the result of competitive pressure, but of the unrecognized consequences of a company's own decisions often made months or years before. If we really want to understand the future of manufacturing, we need to interpret the patterns at work below the *surface of individual events*. And we need to understand how seemingly unrelated factors—a resource constraint, a shift in consumer demand, and a funding decision made several years earlier, for example—can interact, setting off a chain of events that leads to good or bad "fortune" for manufacturing companies, their stakeholders, and their customers.

Consider this example: An obscure auto manufacturing company from a backwater country decides in the 1950s to focus on product and process innovation as its only way to compete. The company sets out to learn everything it can from the giants in the industry, and pioneers many new practices. Quietly and gradually, the company's cars develop a reputation for being easy to run and reliable. By the 1980s, it routinely captures quality awards, which add to its reputation among consumers. By the 2000s, its cachet is so great that its cars command about a 20 percent price premium over competing vehicles of the same size, power, and interior appointments. This premium reflects, in part, a general recognition of higher resale value. When environmental pressures emerge, and automakers must decide what kind of "green" vehicle they can afford to develop, this company—which, of course, is Toyota—captures an early lead.

Some outsiders attribute Toyota's success to just one or two major factors: a pile of cash to invest or innovative technology. But Toyota's greatest advantage has accrued from the way that a number of individual factors—some generated within the company, some external—have all linked together into a virtuous cycle.

Toyota's business model is itself a virtuous cycle. A number of factors are part of it. These include the well-integrated lean production system, the cash flow from the price premium on new cars, the reputation for being able to innovate wisely, the ability to launch new vehicles relatively quickly, and the network of suppliers who systematically work together with Toyota to innovate and lower costs.

The external challenges facing all manufacturers also play a major role in supporting Toyota's virtuous cycle. Environmental pressure has focused consumer and media attention on the first companies to market with green cars; human capital conflicts tend to favor companies like Toyota that have relatively good labor relations; and corporate conflict also confers advantage on companies, again like Toyota, whose senior leadership respects and pursues manufacturing prowess.

Virtuous cycles are rarely perfect and, certainly, Toyota's is not. There are a variety of constraining factors. The company hasn't won the "green car" race by any means, and recent quality issues associated with the launch of Toyota's foray into full-size pickup trucks have shown the difficulties with sustaining rapid expansions. Japan's aging population has created dire labor shortages in that island nation, which have, in turn, impacted the company's ability to fully capitalize on its forays into new technologies.

But virtuous cycles do have this quality: each element that does contribute to the cycle makes the others move faster. At the earliest stages of the cycle, nothing much seems to be happening, but if a company can bring together enough factors that help its business, the momentum gradually builds until, eventually, the enterprise can seem like a bullet train on the track of success.

Of course, internal and external pressures can interact in ways that create the opposite effect, too—a "vicious cycle." Often, an external challenge, such as investor demands for immediate improved returns, will initiate a vicious cycle. Management responds with across-the-board budget cuts, weakening the company's operational position. Another external challenge appears, such as consumer demand for expanded variety, which requires an investment in process innovation, but is throttled by the cost cutting. Revenues drop as consumers turn to competing products, management cuts prices to maintain demand, and a new round of pressure mounts from the investment community. The cycle builds; the company grows weaker and ultimately stumbles publicly. This particular vicious cycle is a common one among manufacturing companies. It is essentially the story of the collapse of Sunbeam, for instance, as told in Chapter 1.

The details of a vicious cycle can vary, but again, one factor tends to be common: challenges—this time, in the form of obstacles and problems that need some kind of fast resolution—cause each other to grow more quickly than they can be managed individually. And, the train becomes a runaway, barreling out of control and often jumping its tracks.

CAN U.S. AUTO MAKERS TRANSFORM THE VICIOUS WAGE CYCLE?

Saddled with uncompetitive wages, overly generous employee benefits, and relatively low-skilled workforces, U.S. automakers have been trapped in a vicious cycle. Yet recent trends suggest that the ultimate outcome could be positive, as a combination of weakened unions, enhanced productivity, and greater manufacturing flexibility promises to close the gap that separates Detroit's cars from those built in low-cost countries such as China.

General Motors, Ford, and Chrysler have long struggled in their competition against foreign automakers such as Honda, Toyota, and Nissan, primarily because of the severe limitations placed on U.S. companies by union agreements. United Auto Workers' wage rates have risen to upward of $75 per hour per employee, including benefits and retiree costs, almost twice as much as the Japanese companies pay. In addition, under the terms of their labor contracts, U.S. automakers have been constrained in their ability to furlough workers when demand falls. This results in excess production that drives down the price of American cars.

Nor have the Big Three been allowed to replace less-educated employees as their job market demographics have shifted. By contrast, foreign automakers have been building plants in the United States staffed with nonunion employees, who receive slightly lower base wages and much reduced benefits compared to the UAW.

The relatively high base wage has enabled "transplant" companies to attract educated workers who are new to the car industry. Many of these hourly workers have two-year certificates, and the skilled maintenance staffers often have college degrees. The education gap between the transplant employees and those in U.S. companies has had a significant impact on factory operations and economics.

Imagine the high level of responsibility for continuous improvement and complex decision making that Toyota can entrust to its workforce.

Imagine, too, the advantages that Honda's new assembly plant—its fourth in the United States—will enjoy when it begins producing cars in 2008 in Indiana, a UAW stronghold. The company has abandoned the practice of setting wage rates in concert with UAW standards. The 2,000 workers at the Indiana plant will have a starting salary of $14.85 an hour, rising to $18.55 in two years, compared to the $28 per hour average base pay of UAW workers at the Big Three assembly plants.

Now, consider the impact that wage and benefits flexibility has on competitiveness. According to a Harbour Report, the average automobile assembly time in the United States is 23 hours. At $75 per hour versus $20 per hour at Hyundai, U.S. companies pay $1,000 to $2,500 more per vehicle. Even compared to Toyota, Nissan, and Honda, the cost gap could be as high as $1,200 per vehicle.

But the makings of cyclical transformation for U.S. automakers appear to be emerging. During 2007 contract negotiations, domestic automakers, led by GM, significantly improved their wage rate position. Not only has GM paid the union to take over its retiree health benefit programs, the automaker also negotiated a two-tier wage scale: new union workers will receive lower wages than existing factory employees for many jobs. In addition, these new workers will not be guaranteed costly defined-benefit pension plans or retiree health-care benefits. This agreement will slash GM's compensation costs to within $10 per hour of Toyota's cost in the United States.

The outlook will continue to improve as GM implements flexibility programs that shift work off assembly lines and align its production closer to market demand. Assuming this and that 30 percent of GM's workers will be new, less expensive hires, over time the automaker's effective wages could drop to around $40 per hour. With an average vehicle production time of 23 hours, these compensation reductions could shave more than $700 off the cost of each GM car.

The impact of this new wage environment will have repercussions in low-cost Asian countries, too. Generally, offshore automobile manufacturing has little to offer except inexpensive workers—a factor that in itself has become less important as automation and lean production practices take hold. A reduction in U.S. wages should seriously erode the economics of manufacturing cars in countries such as China and shipping them to North American markets. The savings in labor will no longer outweigh the logistics costs.

Before the 2007 labor negotiations, GM's car assembly costs in the United States were 150 percent higher than assembling them in China and shipping them to the West. Now, this cost differential has shrunk to only about $100 in China's favor. This amount could be compensated for by the advantages of local U.S. production, such as fast delivery and short, nimble supply chains that would allow U.S. companies to react to changes in demand with more agility than their Asian competitors.

In fact, as these wage alterations take effect, low-cost Asian nations will only be more economical when manufacturing vehicles that have high labor content, such as luxury SUVs. For example, even with Honda's low labor rates, only when a car needs more than 38 hours to make would it be less expensive to produce in China and ship to Detroit than to make in Indiana.

As a final note, currency fluctuations could also play a critical role in the revitalization of U.S. automakers. Indeed, if, as many experts anticipate, the yuan increases in value, then China will be a less significant exporter of vehicles into the United States. This would have an even bigger impact on the competitive dynamics and revitalization of the Detroit-based automakers. Witness the impact of the fall of the dollar between 2001 and 2007 on European automakers. The fall reduced the profitability of exports and has created a growing interest in adding U.S. assembly capacity at companies such as Volkswagen.

BUILDING A CYCLE OF SENSIBILITY

To harness virtuous cycles and avoid vicious ones, the company at the center must develop the kind of managerial sensibility that enables it to appreciate and manage the ways in which external and internal challenges can combine and affect each other, both today and in the future. Developing just such a sensibility starts with recognizing the current and future role of manufacturing in the context of your specific industry, because various pressures combine in ways that manifest themselves very differently from one industry to the next.

For instance, pharmaceutical manufacturers will find themselves continually battered by environmental pressure as many governments and their citizens become increasingly concerned about chemical production issues. But these companies will have only a modicum of trouble retaining and attracting high-quality employees, because on the whole their plants are newer and the nature of the work inside of them is significantly more appealing than in other manufacturing sectors. (One factor that enhances the pharmaceutical work environment, as many workers say, is the relatively even male-to-female ratio.) And while mastering the demands of efficient mass customization will likely require great efforts on the part of many pharma companies, the potential for labor conflicts is likely to be lower because pharma workers tend to earn much more than workers in other industries in their surrounding regions and so have less reason to be dissatisfied.

Alternatively, the challenges that the construction materials industry faces result from a very different set of factors. This sector will have more difficulty finding and recruiting labor given its plant environment, and raw materials will become increasingly expensive as supply dwindles. Most likely, those companies that learn how to harness lean manufacturing, reduce material usage and waste, and make sound process technology choices will gain competitive advantage. Continued consolidation within regions is also likely; the need for efficient and environmentally compliant manufacturers confers an advantage on larger players. At the same time, the relative difficulty of producing some of the industry's semicustomized products in low-cost countries and shipping them long distances will protect some manufacturers from increased competition.

In short, the eight powerful pressures impacting the future of manufacturing, as discussed in Chapter 2, manifest themselves differently among industries (see Exhibit 3-1), even when their average aggregate effect, as seen in the final column, is quite similar.

Nonetheless, it is important to remember the overall lesson of virtuous and vicious cycles. Whatever your industry, the challenges you face as a manufacturing company have an interdependent, reinforcing, collective impact. Like the challenges of the past, they may appear as individual factors that can be dealt with separately before they become a significant headache. And in some cases, that may be possible. For instance, the depth of materials and workforce shortages can be anticipated by demographic and geographic analyses far in advance. And, manufacturers can put in place a variety of measures to prepare for them. For materials shortages, these might include buying options on critically important ingredients

EXHIBIT 3-1 THE IMPACT OF MANUFACTURING'S CHALLENGES, BY INDUSTRY

INDUSTRY APPLICABILITY OF TRENDS

Industry	Environmental pressures	New competition pressures	New customer's demand	Expanding variety demand
Pharmaceuticals	↑	↗	↗	↑
Auto parts	➚	↗	↗	↗
Consumer goods	↗	➚	↗	↑
Chemicals	↑	➚	↗	➚
Construction materials	➚	⇒	➚	➚
Machine building	↗	↗	↗	↗

Industry	Workforce shortages	Material shortages	Management conflict	Labor conflict	TOTAL
Pharmaceuticals	⇒	➚	➚	⇒	↗
Auto parts	↗	↑	➚	↗	↗
Consumer goods	➚	➚	↗	➚	↗
Chemicals	↗	↑	⇒	↗	↗
Construction materials	↗	➚	➚	↗	➚
Machine building	↗	➚	⇒	➚	➚

↑ Entirely different / much stronger than in past

↗ Much different / stronger than in past

➚ Somewhat different / somewhat stronger than in past

⇒ Not much different / not much stronger than in past

Source: Booz Allen Hamilton

or partnering with other companies to develop new sources of supply. For workforce shortages, these might include setting up in-house training programs, automating parts of the operation, or tapping the human capital of other nations.

But any manufacturer that approaches the challenges of the future in traditional piecemeal, one-step-at-a-time fashion will run the risk, now more than ever, of getting caught on a runaway train.

Here is an example from the commercial aerospace industry: Even as customers were eagerly queuing up for newly designed airliners from Airbus and Boeing, the development and production schedules of these planes were plagued and delayed by insufficient parts, components, materials, and technology innovation. In October 2006, Airbus announced a two-year delivery delay on its A380 superjumbo airliner. A year later, Boeing, long expected to hit its deadline, announced a six-month delivery delay on its 787 Dreamliner because of "continued challenges completing assembly of the first airplanes."

Shortages of systems, such as the wire harnesses in an A380, or even shortages of simple parts, such as the rivets needed in a Dreamliner (Exhibit 3-2), sound like relatively minor production issues—easily preventable and even easier to solve. However, when interrelated with other challenges, such as management conflict around manufacturing, difficulties handling new materials and production processes, and the growth of demand in emerging markets, it becomes clearer why these issues surfaced too late in the process, took too long to resolve, and eventually led to questions about the viability of the overall pro-

EXHIBIT 3-2 **BOEING'S DREAMLINER GROUNDED BY RIVETS**

Source: *Photo courtesy of Corbis*

duction philosophies of two major companies. Indeed, there are signs that both companies realize this: Airbus has begun contemplating a less centralized production model that will offload operations to risk-sharing suppliers, and some executives within Boeing are reconsidering its decentralized production constellation.

To name another example, the challenge of expanding variety tends to exacerbate material shortages. This is because mass customization makes the problem of procurement more complex: It's not simply a matter of sourcing a certain material but finding it in a variety of grades, sizes, weights, shapes, colors, and quality levels. In the automotive industry, the explosion of electronic options combined with an increasing number of makes and models has caused the number of different wire harnesses used by a single car maker to rise from a handful to as many as 100. And one missing harness requires that a vehicle be pulled off the line, so now, car manufacturers or their suppliers must hold significantly larger inventories instead of operating just in time.

In fact, in examining the causal relationships between the eight challenges, it is apparent that expanding variety tends to intensify the impact of nearly every other challenge. It exacerbates workforce shortages because more products invariably mean more man-hours per product. It worsens environmental pressures because more stock-keeping units (SKUs) typically translate into more waste. And it creates labor conflict because few worker communities relish the complexity inherent in an ever-expanding product portfolio.

Nevertheless, when production communities try to curtail product variety, they usually face steep uphill battles. The ever-increasing customer focus in most companies tends to make it far easier to add new products than to eliminate them. Even when the economic case is clearly questionable, there is usually a commercial or strategic argument for more variety. Further, the cost accounting associated with expanding variety is often inaccurate, making high-volume products seem more costly than they are and underestimating the costs of new and low-volume products.

Exploring the other side of the cause and effect relationships among the challenges, there is one that tends to be most affected by the others: materials and equipment shortages. This is because the solutions to the other challenges often create additional demands for materials and equipment. Consider manufacturing's needs over the next ten years: In the short term, companies need production shop floor equipment with higher throughputs to meet escalating demand; in the coming three to five years, more versatile manufacturing equipment will be required to satisfy expanding product variety; in ten years, manufacturers will need highly automated equipment that can be operated with the fewest possible workers to overcome workforce shortages. Perhaps the greatest challenge of all is the fact that traditionally, many industries have de-emphasized the value of production technology innovation and held on to manufacturing equipment for anywhere from 15 to 30 years. Now they will have to assign process innovation a new, pivotal role and adopt much tighter equipment obsolescence schedules.

Notably, there is only one challenge that consistently tends to diminish the others—new customer growth. Escalating demand enables economies of scale and utilization, which in turn, inspire expansion in both variety and new technology. This is one reason why organic growth is so prized among companies. Of course, capturing the economies of scale and utilization requires skill and awareness. To profit from the gains inherent in rising demand, sophisticated site volume loading strategies are needed to ensure that utilization levels are maintained or enhanced, too.

Exhibit 3-3 shows how, by understanding the interrelationships between the eight challenges, manufacturers can begin to predict future conditions and enhance the odds of creating and maintaining their own virtuous cycles.

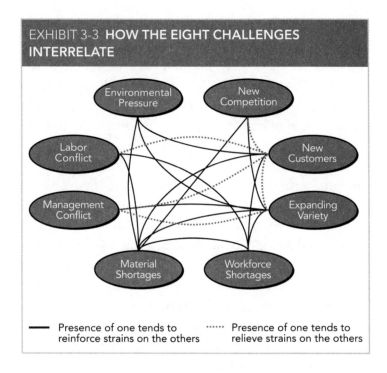

EXHIBIT 3-3 **HOW THE EIGHT CHALLENGES INTERRELATE**

Presence of one tends to reinforce strains on the others

Presence of one tends to relieve strains on the others

MANUFACTURING RESILIENCE: FINANCE AND STRATEGY

The interdependent nature of the eight challenges helps to explain why, for virtually all manufacturers, a significant financial commitment is not only an important component in creating virtuous cycles but often critical to their very survival. The problems that stem from the relationships among the challenges defy simple fixes. Rather, they demand that manufacturers evolve—making full use of the positive outcomes from those trends, such as expanding variety and new customers, that can help fuel the necessary growth.

And to be sure, proactive investment in manufacturing represents a paradigm shift for many companies in which any voluntary funding of the function is seen as tantamount to *over*investment. In fact, many companies are determinedly cost- and investment-shy when it comes to manufacturing, spending the bare minimum on their factories and hoping all the while for easy, inexpensive fixes that will enable them to work faster and smarter. Investment in process R&D among the Global Fortune 500 industrial companies has decreased significantly as a percentage of sales in the past two decades. However, the manufacturing capital expenditure earmarked for upgrading equipment has barely budged in the past decade; in a sample of 17 multinationals, we found an increase of barely 1.5 percent above invested capital.

This underinvestment in manufacturing assets will become increasingly dangerous as the challenges intensify. It is already catching up with some companies. One typical example involves an industrial materials producer that was acquired by a financial holding company. Although it was located exclusively in high-labor-cost locations, in the past the company had pioneered new production technologies that enabled it to replace almost 35 percent of the manual labor per ton produced through automation and yield increases. Under worsened financial circumstances, however, the new ownership blocked investment in innovative equipment. For several years, a series of "quick-fix" solutions, including staff reductions, appeared to help turn the business around, but ultimately the quick fixes were exhausted, Asian competitors won over longstanding customers, and the company collapsed.

Manufacturers who hope to harness the power of virtuous cycles will have to craft new strategies that focus on gaining competitive advantage versus maintaining their current positions or incremental improvement. Quick fixes do not warrant investment; integrated manufacturing and product strategies that make it possible to consistently win more volume and higher returns do.

There is no question that these strategies will have to funnel more money into revamping and recreating production processes so that they are better aligned to respond to the eight challenges, whether that means consuming more environmentally sound materials, converting to more abundant materials, designing a more efficient way to handle product variation and complexity, or replacing the need for manual labor. Manufacturers will also have to provide the funding needed to repair or replace aging manufacturing infrastructure, auxiliary equipment, such as conveyors, air conditioning units, and warehousing and storage systems. These seemingly uncritical assets are reaching breaking point in many locations.

In many companies, this will require a new set of financial capabilities for and within the manufacturing function. At the heart of this requirement is the need for manufacturing leaders to learn new skills. Manufacturing and operations chiefs will need to learn to develop appropriation requests and allocate money more wisely, to stage investments that build toward long-term goals, and to draw upon the expertise of other functions, such as R&D and finance, to help bolster the anticipated returns on manufacturing investments. Such skills will become de rigueur for manufacturing leaders who must learn to better compete for funding that is often directed to other compelling priorities, such as product innovation, systems integration, and geographical expansion.

Major strategic questions, such as how much to invest in manufacturing and where to invest and how rapidly, are going to be more difficult to answer than in the past, too. There will almost certainly not be stock answers to these questions. And those companies that simply emulate their competitors' spending will condemn themselves to also-ran positions in their industries. Instead, the answers will have to be, in large part, unique to each company, and reaching them will require profound internal analysis.

Unfortunately, this represents another level of strategic capability that is beyond the norm in most manufacturing companies. Most companies, for example, produce rosy forecasts of future volumes and pricing to validate their current plans, knowing that they probably won't be held accountable in the long term. As a result, when investments in automation and process technology, manufacturing footprint changes, and other substantial projects are proposed, this inherently exaggerated baseline ensures that the anticipated return on improvement is minimized. And the investments, no matter how worthy, are less likely to be approved.

Even among Fortune 500 manufacturers, many companies do not allocate more than a handful of dedicated personnel to crafting, charting, exploring, and adjusting the function's strategies. Moreover, there is almost no manufacturing-literate staff—often none whatsoever—within the business development and strategy functions of those same companies.

This can and sometimes does translate into a vicious cycle. The competitive, market, and internal portraits are not painted accurately, and thus, when expectations are not met, a crisis of confidence in the manufacturing strategy develops. Investment is withheld. As a result, plants that require significant upgrades become less and less competitive, those that should be shuttered drive down utilization throughout the network, and the implementation of process technologies is dragged out over years to the point of irrelevance. Down and down it goes.

One quality that all sound manufacturing strategies share is resilience. Resilience is the organizational counterpart to resourcefulness in an individual: the ability to foresee problems, anticipate solutions, and adapt on the fly to sudden difficulties, particularly when they come from the intersections of trends. After years of neglecting their manufacturing functions, many companies have lost this resilience. Take today's materials shortages, for example. Many manufacturers have plans in place for alternative sources for these materials, but there are far fewer companies that can say how and how quickly they could replace those materials altogether and even fewer that are bringing new production processes that could work without them onstream.

Procter & Gamble is a company that has repeatedly demonstrated the quality of resilience in its innovative abilities vis-à-vis manufacturing equipment engineering. P&G's approach exemplifies the philosophy that product innovation is inherently more fragile than process innovation. The company maintains a well-integrated team of engineers and manufacturers who steer its equipment development process. The company maintains an advantaged network of largely low-cost but highly capable machine builders located in countries such as Brazil and

China that produce "build-to-print" components for P&G's proprietary manufacturing lines. As a result, P&G is well ahead of its competitors in process machine-building skills. In fact, we estimate it has at least a three-to-four-year and tens-of-millions-of-dollars leg up in this

RESILIENCE: A PALPABLE FEELING IN THE WORKPLACE

It's hardly scientific, but you can sense manufacturing resilience by mood and undercurrents in the workplace. It is present in the trust that the company's executives have in the targets that manufacturing commits to and by their level of engagement in both day-to-day operations and plans for the future on the shop floor. It can be seen in the attitude that support functions exhibit toward manufacturing: highly responsive and supportive of manufacturing goals and willing to subordinate their own agendas. IT, for instance, does not push Enterprise Resource Planning (ERP) modules solely for the sake of standardization but helps to develop and roll out top-flight software solutions to help manufacturing achieve its strategic goals. Resilience is palpably visible within the engineering staff, which is excited and open to collaboration in pursuit of enhanced manufacturability and new manufacturing ideas. They are also ready and eager to display the technical horsepower needed to generate inventive automation and production equipment solutions. All of these psychological attributes contribute to manufacturing resilience.

R&D-based skill set. This competitive advantage could in itself be enough to set companies like P&G on the road to "make" rather than "break."

"MAKE OR BUY" IS A "MAKE-OR-BREAK" DECISION

Many companies have already tried (and it is likely that more will try) to navigate the challenges that dominate the manufacturing agenda by passing some or all of their production operations to another company: in other words, by outsourcing.

Some companies choose an "all-buy" solution and outsource every aspect of the manufacturing process for a particular brand or business unit. Nike is a well-known pioneer of this strategy. Less familiar examples include beer maker Samuel Adams, Kraft Foods, and Apple Computer. Sam Adams Cherry Wheat, Polly-O Mozzarella, and iPods are not all made by the companies whose logos they sport. Many companies farm out only the noncore elements of their manufacturing operations and continue to perform the final assembly and other essential tasks in house. Boeing and Airbus are both pursuing this strategy with various degrees of intensity.

Outsourcing, especially when it involves offshoring, is a highly politicized, and often demonized, practice. But outsourcing can contribute to virtuous as well as vicious cycles, and neither full nor partial outsourcing solutions are inherently wrong. In fact, there are manufacturers in every industry who make the mistake of producing parts or products that are more economically and efficiently outsourced—particularly those items that contain very little intellectual property and require almost no innovation prowess to produce. In many of these cases, outside contractors can do the work at higher scale and lower wages, with little risk of losing valuable process innovation opportunities or product launch robustness. Outsourcing under these conditions can cut a company's costs significantly and free up additional capital that can be reinvested in improving the efficiency and output of core operations.

Consider the case of the German agricultural equipment maker Claas. Although Claas manufactures what some have called "the Rolls Royce of harvesting equipment," at around the turn of the millennium its senior leaders realized the company's reputation for high-quality machinery was in danger of being eclipsed by the scale advantages enjoyed by its primary competitors, some of which were ten times its size. They realized that because the 90-year-old company had stayed true to its roots in central Germany, it was incurring the greater costs inherent in Western factories. To address this imbalance, Claas devised a manufacturing strategy dubbed "roll-up from the bottom." Under this plan, upstream metalworking activities that were labor intensive and not particularly innovative or differentiating were outsourced to Eastern European suppliers. Meanwhile, Claas's management team refocused its resources and attention on product development as well as downstream assembly activities, which were streamlined using "fish-bone" analyses and quick changeover techniques. In part because of this initiative, Claas's net income more than doubled between 2002 and 2006, rising from 32.5 million euros to 80.9 million euros.

EXHIBIT 3-4 LEGO'S EXPANDED PLANT IN THE CZECH REPUBLIC

Source: *Photo courtesy of the Lego Group*

In another example of efficient outsourcing, the Lego Group, in 2005, expanded its plant in the Czech Republic (Exhibit 3-4) and outsourced work to a global contractor with a plant in Hungary rather than send more of its production to low-cost Chinese manufacturers. Why? Among other reasons, production in Eastern Europe reaches store shelves in Western Europe in just a few days compared to weeks from Chinese factories—a crucial time advantage given that the European market accounts for 60 percent of Lego's revenue and 40 percent of the Danish company's toy sales take place during the Christmas season.

What manufacturers need is a measured and resilient outsourcing strategy that takes into account the challenges they face and the needs of the virtuous cycles they are trying to create. Unfortunately, if the bulk of today's outsourcing decisions are any indication, creative and constructive approaches to sourcing will remain relatively rare. All too many outsourcing decisions are driven by knee-jerk reactions characterized by naïveté or short-termism and aimed at avoidance. In many of these cases, management has lost confidence in manufacturing's ability to deliver improvement, based in turn on assessments of its capabilities and on the experience of past problems. Thus, companies literally wash their hands of their manufacturing problems by ceding them to low-cost "specialists." In those organizations, outsourcing often turns out to be a momentarily expedient, stopgap solution. These stopgaps eventually fail because they haven't been well thought out.

A better approach is to use a rigorous process to decide whether outsourcing is the best option. Rather than base decisions on, for example, the estimated cost of in-house manufacturing versus the variable costs associated with outsourced manufacturing plus shipping and a few contingency expenses, outsourcing strategists should take into account the unexpected and hidden costs of outsourcing and the potential gains of in-house production. Many of these gains may not yet be realized.

One often-unanticipated cost is the expense related to quality control. The repair and/or replacement of products that fall below standard requirements—a not uncommon result in cases where a supplier is coming up to speed on complex parts or the workforce is relatively unskilled and inexperienced—can add significant costs. And, of course, there are the time and travel expenses involved in flying managers to distant locales to solve such problems.

Other hidden costs include the added complexity that outsourcing creates in a manufacturing network and its

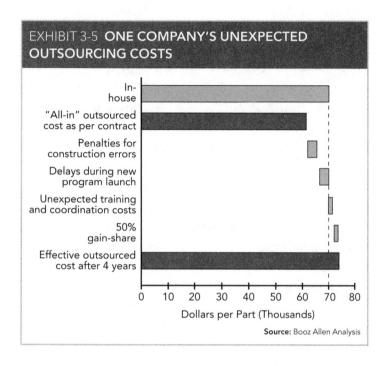

EXHIBIT 3-5 **ONE COMPANY'S UNEXPECTED OUTSOURCING COSTS**

Source: Booz Allen Analysis

effect on a company's ability to maintain lean flows of material and information within its value chain. Integrating product development between engineering units and outsourcers can be particularly problematic. When a product development team loses touch with outsourced production, then the design for manufacturability, preproduction approval processes, and cycle time (both overall cycle time and that used for critical changes) frequently suffer. Issues such as the impact of changes on contractual terms interfere with frank, open problem solving.

As shown in Exhibit 3-5, when one aerospace company analyzed the impact of unexpected costs like those discussed above, it discovered that its outsourced airframe parts were more expensive than the in-house production they had replaced. And as it turned out, it was not possible to reverse its decision in the short term and extremely hard in the medium term.

Outsourcing problems like these are exacerbated when manufacturers outsource high-variety, low-volume parts and products and keep the easy, less-expensive items with predictable production schedules in house. This is not uncommon because manufacturing managers typically relish the prospect of outsourcing low-volume, complex units that are harder on the manufacturing processes and negatively impact "one size fits all" performance metrics. (Low-volume parts drive up "cost-per-unit" statistics and overhead costs because of the greater setup time, more engineering required, more difficult production planning, and usually higher quality control costs.) But in choosing this strategy, they often outsource the same problems to another company, in addition to creating longer lead times in items whose demand is more difficult to predict. As a result, rush orders and expedited shipping become a common occurrence and costs escalate accordingly. Moreover, when a "rushed" part or product has a quality problem, there is no quick recourse. Problems like this can quickly become vicious cycles in which customers become more and more disgruntled while days are wasted in transit, there is wrangling about responsibility, and production must be reprogrammed. In fact, highly variable parts and products can be a competitive advantage instead of a headache for many producers, because they require the development of flexible systems and support local operations. If this fits a company's business model, then it should be pursuing the capability to manage such complexity (perhaps by outsourcing high-volume parts and products and keeping the low-volume items in house). Nike's 2003 decision to make its customized backpacks in San Francisco instead of China fits this description. The company apparently realized that the lower labor and capital costs associated with outsourcing were offset by the logistics of importing goods and consequent lost sales and overstocks that would be caused by delivery delays.

Finally, selling off existing operations in the shift to an outsourcing strategy can also be difficult. Witness a recent incident involving a $20+ billion engineered products company. After the company decided to sell its chronically underperforming parts factories, a number of investment banks were hired to oversee the sale of the plants. But the process hit a major snag when the only serious buyers turned out to be a low-cost competitor wishing to get access to the company's technology, a large supplier to the company's main competitor who wanted to monopolize the supply base and would likely favor the competitor, and a subscale new entrant to the business. The company's leaders were forced to reverse course and now are struggling to save a manufacturing operation that they had intended to abandon.

MAKE OR BREAK: THE CHINA STORY

In a few short decades, Chinese manufacturing has evolved from a far-fetched idea to a global juggernaut. Yet, as was revealed in a 2008 American Chamber of Commerce/Booz Allen Hamilton survey of 500 companies with plants in China's three major industrial zones, these manufacturers (92 percent of which are foreign-owned or joint venture operations) are subject to the same challenges in China as manufacturers elsewhere.

For all the talk of manufacturing jobs migrating to China, the survey revealed that more companies located their plants in that nation to fulfill burgeoning demand in its domestic markets than to tap into its sea of low-cost labor (71 percent versus 61 percent). Further, although there is no doubt that China remains an attractive choice for very large scale, low-labor-cost operations, 56 percent of respondents believe that manufacturing in China's three large industrial zones is already losing its economic appeal.

This surprising development is being driven by the same challenges faced by the West. For one thing, 63 percent of the survey's respondents believe that China's labor cost advantage is fast shifting to other low-cost nations, such as Vietnam, India, and Indonesia. They also see corresponding shifts in the supply of skilled labor and management talent, which is perceived to be higher in other Asian nations, particularly India. Several local Indian companies, such as Bharat Forge (a maker of forged car parts) and Sundaram (a fastener maker), have become preferred suppliers to the world's top automakers while the auto supply market has few Chinese players of the same status.

China's intellectual property (IP) and legal environment is also impacting its competitiveness; 37 percent of the respondents feel that other Asian countries have better IP and legal environments. IP violations, ranging from counterfeit IKEA furniture (sold under the brand name "IDEA") to Chery Automobile Company's QQ minicar (which is virtually a twin of the Chevrolet Spark), remain a serious issue. It is no surprise that China's legal framework is perceived to be weak and immature, as many of the laws and legal proceedings around the protection of intellectual property are relatively new.

As is shown in Exhibit 3-6, China still enjoys advantages over its emerging competitors, including a more developed supply base, better logistics infrastructure, and the huge domestic market. Nevertheless, more than half of the survey respondents judge the supply base in China to be of insufficient capability. Interestingly, 26 percent assign better supply ratings to other Asian nations. In fact, some smaller Asian countries are not too far behind Europe and the United States in this regard. The same number (26 percent) of respondents also believes that the cost and supply of raw materials can be superior in other Asian nations.

The emergence of the Indian subcontinent as another market of impressive size served by a rapidly developing infrastructure particularly affects the perception of China's advantages. In fact, when asked about their preferred destinations for relocation, the survey respondents ranked India first, followed by Vietnam, Thailand, and Malaysia.

To be sure, India and China are viewed as critical locations for the very reason that both have such

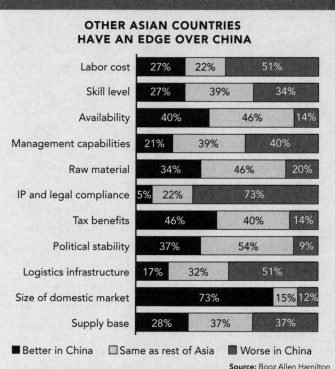

EXHIBIT 3-6 PERCEPTIONS OF THE MANUFACTURING ENVIRONMENT IN CHINA'S THREE INDUSTRIAL ZONES VS. OTHER LOW-COST ASIAN NATIONS

OTHER ASIAN COUNTRIES HAVE AN EDGE OVER CHINA

Category	Better in China	Same as rest of Asia	Worse in China
Labor cost	27%	22%	51%
Skill level	27%	39%	34%
Availability	40%	46%	14%
Management capabilities	21%	39%	40%
Raw material	34%	46%	20%
IP and legal compliance	5%	22%	73%
Tax benefits	46%	40%	14%
Political stability	37%	54%	9%
Logistics infrastructure	17%	32%	51%
Size of domestic market	73%	15%	12%
Supply base	28%	37%	37%

■ Better in China   □ Same as rest of Asia   ■ Worse in China

Source: Booz Allen Hamilton

large market potential. For automotive suppliers, it is almost unimaginable not to be operating in China, and a similar situation is quickly developing in India.

Exacerbating the external pressure on the competitiveness of China's three industrial zones is a second major threat: the dearth of modern manufacturing systems in its factories. In general, the companies in the survey have not leveraged state-of-the-art thinking in their plants, 72 percent of which are greenfields established within the past five years.

Sales forecasting and demand planning, for example, are largely based only on experience (as opposed to more effective analysis), and 70 percent of respondents agree that their own forecasting processes are far too rudimentary. This may explain why Chinese industry overall has surprisingly high inventories. They also have yet to reap the benefits of manufacturing paradigms, such as lean production, Six Sigma, and TPM; 43 percent stated that they were not ready to adopt these methodologies, and 34 percent said they were planning only partial implementations. This suggests a short-term mindset that may ultimately erode China's remaining advantages. Companies in countries such as South Korea and India are generally farther along the lean road. It is noteworthy that more Indian than Chinese manufacturers have won the Deming Award (for quality management) in recent years.

The third major threat to the competitiveness of China's three industrial zones is also close at hand. Shanghai, Beijing, and Guangzhou remain China's top business centers, but their economies are overheated, operational costs are rising, and most manufacturers do not find them to be the most attractive choices for relocation any longer. In fact, when asked to pick a new manufacturing location within China, the survey respondents choose the Yangtze River Delta region, Pearl Delta region, Bohai Delta region,

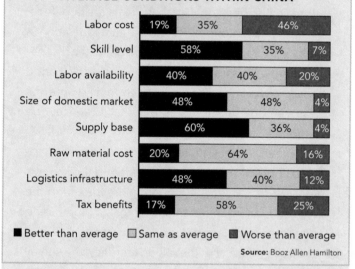

EXHIBIT 3-7 **PERCEPTIONS OF THE MANUFACTURING ENVIRONMENT IN THE THREE INDUSTRIAL ZONES VS. OTHER REGIONS WITHIN CHINA**

COMPETITIVENESS OF DESIRED LOCATION (WITHIN CHINA) AGAINST THAT OF AVERAGE CONDITIONS WITHIN CHINA

	Better than average	Same as average	Worse than average
Labor cost	19%	35%	46%
Skill level	58%	35%	7%
Labor availability	40%	40%	20%
Size of domestic market	48%	48%	4%
Supply base	60%	36%	4%
Raw material cost	20%	64%	16%
Logistics infrastructure	48%	40%	12%
Tax benefits	17%	58%	25%

■ Better than average □ Same as average ■ Worse than average

Source: Booz Allen Hamilton

Northwestern areas and other coastal areas as the front runners for relocation.

In fact, 54 percent of those surveyed say that four of these lesser-known locations within China offer a less-expensive pool of labor. Compared to the three established industrial zones, 58 percent of respondents have found that the skills and quality of the labor pools in these alternative areas are better, and 80 percent believe the availability of labor is the same or better (see Exhibit 3-7). These perceptions represent a serious threat to the competitiveness of

China's existing manufacturing hubs, and many companies are already contemplating relocation from Shanghai, Beijing, and Guangzhou to these lesser-known areas as well as to neighboring Asian countries.

Manufacturers in China expect to face additional future challenges, too. But these fears are largely related to macroeconomic factors. That expectation in itself may be a threat, because the belief that manufacturing success is dependent on economic conditions discourages the introspection and internal improvement that enables manufacturers to ride economic waves.

What are these fears? The fear of currency appreciation is at the top of the list among the survey's respondents. Given the mounting pressure from the World Trade Organization and China's major trading partners (including the United States) to address the country's artificially undervalued currency, the survey respondents believe it is only a matter of time before China will be forced to adopt monetary reforms that diminish its competitiveness.

The next most dreaded factor is inflationary pressure. With the middle class expanding and rising prosperity, China's consumer economy is primed for inflation, and increasing prices will not serve manufacturers' interests. It may be counterintuitive for outsiders, but the survey respondents also worry about how China's potential movement away from authoritarian government could impact the competitiveness of their operations in the country.

Wage increases and anemic employee retention rates are problems waiting in the wings. There is a shortage of skilled manufacturing labor in China, and that is clearly reflected in the fact that manufacturing wages doubled between 1997 and 2006. Further, almost all respondents see their blue-collar workers as uncommitted to their companies and ready to defect at the offer of the slightest increase in wages. This probably has some foundation in fact. Many of these workers migrated to the three industrial areas solely to earn higher wages and do not have the family and community ties that support workforce stability.

Finally, manufacturers perceive the protectionist trade policies of the United States and European Union to be hostile to China. In fact, protectionism has been a growing trend and is likely to continue. This may, of course, negatively affect the competitiveness of the manufacturing sector.

In spite of these real and perceived challenges to China's prime industrial areas, the overall opportunity for manufacturing success remains enormous. The combination of low wages and huge market potential will likely continue. But there is an urgent message between the lines of the survey: Chinese manufacturers must improve efficiency and upgrade practices soon, before their key advantage of cost shifts elsewhere. The choice, for an increasing number of Chinese manufacturers, like manufacturers everywhere, will be "make" or "break."

THE RISE OF THE INTEGRATOR

The increasing popularity of outsourcing among manufacturers has given rise to "manufacturing integrators." These contract manufacturers swallow up many unwanted factories, consolidate their production processes, and then produce and ship finished items for manufacturers. Integrating the manufacturing operations of multiple producers/competitors creates greater scale and enhances process technology and capacity utilization, a fact proven by the tremendous cost reductions achieved over the years by integrators in the electronics sector.

In many cases, manufacturers turn to these companies to help them restructure their supply base and act as Tier 1 integrators. Typical of such ventures was Airbus's decision during its 2007 restructuring to sell, instead of shutter, noncore plants—including Meaulte in France, Varel and Nordenham in Germany, and Filton in the United Kingdom—in the hopes of attracting integrators who would become long-term partners. As fears about quality, hidden costs, and rising wages in low-cost nations drive a backlash against outsourcing, more and more manufacturing facilities will likely become candidates for this kind of arrangement.

Integrators are not new. The concept made its debut decades ago in the shipping industry, when United Kingdom–based Tibbett & Britten purchased warehouses from consumer goods firms and created an outbound logistics network that they all shared.

Not long after that, integrators surfaced in the electronics manufacturing industry. The two largest integrators, Solectron and Flextronics (now a merged company), controlled a substantial share of all electronics subcomponent manufacturing by 2000, when they shifted most of their operations to low-cost nations. Then, the dot-com crash, which hit especially hard at many of the telecommunications and computer hardware companies that purchased components from Solectron and Flextronics, substantially slowed their growth.

Meanwhile, in the pharmaceutical industry, contracting out chemicals production to integrators like Switzerland's Lonza and the Netherlands' DSM became fashionable as a way to meet burgeoning demand. In this case, overinvestment resulted in excess capacity among pharmaceutical integrators, who were forced to start scrambling for contracts. This situation worsened as generics and meager new product pipelines reduced demand.

Given these past problems, the current wave of integrators is trying new models. In some cases, they are starting as factory operations spun off by traditional manufacturing companies; now they make components and

> With a few exceptions, integrators usually play a limited role in most industries. Even in the most integrator-friendly industries, they account for less than 4 percent of output, and they tend to focus on less complex, less value-added parts. In general, they do run top-notch manufacturing operations—indeed, they view manufacturing excellence as their core skill and, because of economies of scale and consolidation, they can offer high-quality products at the lowest cost.

parts for their former parent company's competitors as well. In others, private equity firms are stepping up to the plate. For example, Canada's Onex Corporation recently bought two large Boeing plants, instantly becoming one of the world's largest aerospace suppliers.

Unhappily, many companies sell or divest manufacturing to integrators without fully considering the implications. When a company is anxious to move on, it may sell its manufacturing assets too quickly. When the number of qualified integrators is small, this can lead to poor transaction prices.

Furthermore, price setting with integrators often can be problematic. Integrators tend to raise their prices, knowing that switching to a new integrator requires a Herculean effort on the part of their customers. This high switching cost is driven by the fact that the current integrator often has a significant advantage over new suppliers in terms of having the equipment, process experience, and tooling already in place; conversely, a new supplier will likely incur high start-up costs and some quality issues during start-up. "Cost plus" arrangements are an alternative to set prices, but they are not very effective either. The integrator has no incentive to reduce costs, and thus the burden to manage costs shifts back to the customer, who now has little or no control over the manufacturing operation.

Manufacturers also tend to forget that the integrator's *raison d'être* is to work for many companies—usually competitors who use similar manufacturing technologies. Aside from the potential exposure of intellectual property, which can be minimized if the divesting firm gives the integrator only nonproprietary or noncritical products and processes, there is a constant battle for priority attention (who comes first in the delivery sequence) and new investment (how quickly integrators will commit capital for new product lines). Integrators can become direct competitors, too. Th. Goldschmitt AG (now the Chemical business unit of Evonik Industries) is a chemicals contract manufacturer of (among other things) surfactants that are used in detergents and shampoos. When one of its largest customers decided to in-source production, the company had only one way to remain a viable enterprise: it forward-integrated and began selling products directly to end customers.

In addition to divesting operations to integrators, some companies are partnering with their competitors to jointly manage and optimize their manufacturing networks. In the petrochemicals industry, it is commonplace for companies to forge short-term swap arrangements. For example, rival A will offer refinery capacity in Turkey to rival B, who wishes to deliver ethylene to the Middle East market, in return for use of rival B's ethylene capacity in Rotterdam to facilitate its own northern European shipments. Typically, these arrangements are made to minimize transportation time and costs, as well as to avoid overcapacity. There are similar nascent examples of manufacturing alliances in other industries—for example in outdoor equipment and kitchen supplies—but they are still rare. These arrangements can also be beneficial for small companies that feel they do not have the bargaining clout needed to deal with contract manufacturers or integrators.

As with outsourcing, joint competitive arrangements are problematic in that they dilute the ability of companies to differentiate themselves. While it can be argued that off-loading manufacturing makes sense for products that are clear commodities with established processes, that isn't necessarily true. After all, there are no static products and processes, and proprietary manufacturing advances often can create a new set of competitive advantages. In fact, innovations in seemingly mature manufacturing processes such as ethanol and certain food ingredient biogums have revived the growth and fortunes of a number of companies. At J.D. Irving, a Canadian firm whose factories were for years focused on mature commodity sectors like pulp and lumber, fermentation-based processes enabled reignition of manufacturing operations around the production of ethanol. Breakthroughs like these don't occur at companies that abdicate their place in the future of manufacturing.

THE MANUFACTURING TRANSFORMATION

The final alternative is to become one's own integrator: to invest in manufacturing prowess and use a well-considered combination of in-house and outsourced operations to navigate the eight challenges and create virtuous cycles. Manufacturers who follow such a course could remain competitive in terms of costs *and* maintain control of core manufacturing operations.

The decision about where to manufacture and how to incorporate outsourcing, integrators, and investment into a manufacturing strategy will ultimately be determined by the economics of reaching customers. For example, building products, such as windows, doors, and skylights, among others, are likely to continue to be made where they will be used, primarily because they are semicustomized, have very precise delivery dates and short lead times, and are expensive to ship. Meanwhile, other building products, including a wide variety of plumbing products, lighting, bathroom fixtures and hardware, are rapidly moving to low-cost countries. Certain automobile parts that are difficult to ship, such as instrument panels, seats, and gas tanks, are likely to remain localized as well. But again, by shifting the production of many parts to poorer countries, automakers in high-cost countries can compete as effectively as manufacturers with low-cost country assets.

What will it take to create a virtuous cycle in this game of world-class manufacturing? The "table stakes" are the recognition of manufacturing's critical role and a willingness to invest in labor and management talent, production systems, process innovation, capital equipment, and so on.

But thus far, the corporate track record in transforming manufacturing operations is not entirely encouraging (see Exhibit 3-8). Success rates—defined as a 15 percent improvement in 18 months that is sustained thereafter— generally hover around 40 percent. These rates are even lower when the transformation requires the cooperation and commitment of shop floor communities. Indeed, the reality may be worse than the statistics suggest, for two reasons: First, these rates only relate to the achievement of targets set by the companies themselves and don't account for the fact that these targets may be set well below their full potential. Second, these success rates are only for selected components of manufacturing transformations; aggregate success rates for holistic transformations are arguably much lower.

In the past, for many companies, it hasn't mattered much that their manufacturing function has underperformed

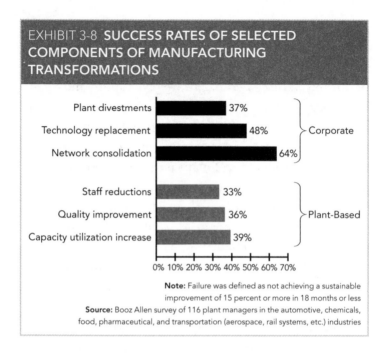

EXHIBIT 3-8 **SUCCESS RATES OF SELECTED COMPONENTS OF MANUFACTURING TRANSFORMATIONS**

Note: Failure was defined as not achieving a sustainable improvement of 15 percent or more in 18 months or less

Source: Booz Allen survey of 116 plant managers in the automotive, chemicals, food, pharmaceutical, and transportation (aerospace, rail systems, etc.) industries

and left millions or even billions of dollars or euros or yen worth of value untapped. Many companies have survived anyway. However, the manufacturing challenges of the past were child's play compared to the vicious cycles that could develop in the coming 15 to 20 years. To avoid them, manufacturers must raise their game by a factor of 2 or 3. Those that do—that double or triple their annual process R&D investments and capital expenditures to maintain and upgrade their operations, that double or triple the attention and patience of senior executives toward the function, and that double or triple the intelligence and effort they apply to creating innovative systems of solutions rather than one-off fixes—will own the future of manufacturing.

MBCI BUILDS A VIRTUOUS CYCLE

There are no easy answers to the challenges facing manufacturing, and those challenges are likely to become more substantial in the coming years, not less. But this situation harbors a huge opportunity for both large, global companies and relatively small, locally focused manufacturers. Witness the performance of MasterBrand Cabinets, Inc. (MBCI), a subsidiary of Fortune Brands based in Jasper, Indiana (about 200 miles south of Chicago). In the U.S. kitchen cabinet business, MBCI has chosen a path that carefully considers products and product complexity, low-cost countries versus domestic manufacturing, the number of plants and their mission, and perhaps most important, the way it manufactures products in each of its plants.

Kitchen cabinets used to be a largely localized business in which cabinetmakers with small independent factories served a town or city. Then, the combined effect of the explosion of the big-box retailer and the application of scaled manufacturing solutions enabled the three largest players to capture over 60 percent of the market. In the year 2000, another trend developed: low-cost Chinese products began to show up at the major kitchen and bath shows, represented by the major distributors.

MBCI CEO Rich Forbes and his management team dove into the potential threat and discovered that they could beat the imports, but only by using a systematic approach to gain advantage at every point in the value stream. For hardware and doors, for example, the team determined that outsourcing production to low-cost countries could eliminate significant labor cost and still be relatively inexpensive to ship. Furthermore, certain species of wood were less expensive in certain low-cost regions, and hand sanding was economically viable in these regions, too. They realized that they could offer a better quality product at a lower price.

They also identified limitations to outsourcing. Making and finishing all doors in China, for instance, could cause problems. MBCI would have to hold too much inventory of the slower running products; it would be difficult to provide immediate response to customer requests; and depending on regulations (and the vagaries of supply and demand), wood costs could vary considerably.

The team found the right answer for MBCI in a mixed sourcing model. Using China, Mexico, and nine core plants in the United States (at lower production rates), the company reduced its total costs, while preserving industry-leading service levels and maintaining the flexibility needed to react to changes in the economics. It started up a new plant in Mexico, which insourced production that MBCI had previously purchased from outside suppliers, and it outsourced some high-volume doors to Chinese producers. At the same time, it maintained the ability to handle low-volume doors that the market demanded and to service urgent response requirements with its domestic plants.

MBCI did not stop there. In the final assembly of cabinets, the company found that closeness to the end customer outweighed many other effects in view of the high shipping costs. So, it established lead times of 2-to-14 days on made-to-order cabinets. This industry-leading delivery promise effectively created a value proposition that no overseas producer could match and was actually more responsive than many local producers. In many segments, especially builders, this service level was a major competitive advantage.

MBCI's CEO also led a major effort to standardize the processes within each plant and drive for continuous improvement. The results: improved quality, inventory reduction, and costs held in check. On top of the manufacturing improvements, MBCI launched hundreds of new variations through its product lines, aimed at giving customers and designers exactly what they wanted. For instance, popular new multi-step finishes, including glazes, were introduced.

The market has rewarded these moves, but the expanded variety in wood species, finishes, interior effects, and sizes resulted in exponential growth in product complexity. MBCI is now studying how to manage that complexity within its plants and is considering tailoring its production footprint and product launch strategy accordingly.

Today, MBCI has a complex product line and a

tailored plant and supply chain structure that delivers an excellent value compared to overseas competition. Its product and service level cannot be matched without a domestic footprint. It was a company sitting in the cross-hairs of manufacturing's challenges, but it responded by creating a virtuous cycle that has enabled it to more than triple sales over nine years to approximately $2 billion.

For notes and resources visit our Web site:
www.businessfuture.com

4

PLANNING FOR SUCCESS

SUCCESS IN manufacturing begins with a deceptively simple idea: for a manufacturer to be competitive, manufacturing must be appreciated. A great manufacturing strategy has its own particular dynamics: It takes long-term investment, a valued voice in the strategic direction of the enterprise, and a practice of involving people at every level in process innovation and improvement. Companies may find it counterintuitive, these days, to treat manufacturing capability as a strategic core asset—equal in importance to marketing, finance, sales, or innovation—but those who do have a natural advantage in a make-or-break world.

Consider Procter & Gamble: Despite the fact that P&G treats every major new manufacturing project as a make-or-buy decision, relatively little of its manufacturing is outsourced. Approval for each new product, new plant, and new plant extension requires the manufacturing function to show a demonstrable advantage versus competitors and contract manufacturers. After P&G's manufacturing community has passed an idea through this first gate, it remains under constant scrutiny. For example, one typical shop floor metric tracks production cost per unit against competitors. The purpose of this exercise is to plumb the state of the art to determine if anyone else can produce these items more efficiently and with a higher degree of quality and reliability than P&G's in-house teams (which themselves have been at the forefront of manufacturing expertise for more than 40 years). On a nearly continuous basis, P&G's internal manufacturing communities compare their performance to external bidders and prove that they are operating at or very near best-in-class levels.

Because it appreciates the value delivered by manufacturing, and because of its ingrained knowledge of manufacturing capability, P&G can make bolder, longer-term investment decisions than its competitors. These decisions might include developing or purchasing manufacturing equipment that can produce higher yields or operate with more streamlined changeovers. They might include investing in greater flexibility to accommodate new products, or in modular product and production-shop designs that enable easy repair and the quick relocation of factory capacity. The experience from these investments then further improves the function's performance, reinforces the manufacturing mindset, and enhances the success rates of improvement programs—a virtuous cycle in its own right.

Unfortunately, P&G is something of a rarity among manufacturers. Most companies find it difficult to discern the performance improvements and gains that manufacturing delivers. This may well be because the manufacturing function (unlike others such as marketing or R&D) is characterized by

➤ Long periods of stability in which repetitive processes churn out identical products day in and day out.

➤ Inaccessibility to the corporate hierarchy: most manufacturing operations take place in plants far from headquarters.

➤ Isolation from the outside world: manufacturing is not customer-facing and is often kept separate from suppliers.

In fact, these characteristics often cause manufacturing to be mistaken for a relatively nonstrategic function, much like a "back office" function such as payroll. But the lifespan of even the most stagnant manufacturing enterprise is punctuated by moments of change: defining decision points that can make or break an enterprise. These moments can occur at any time, and they distinguish manufacturing from other less mission-critical functions.

These moments often occur when new products or new production technologies are launched. A manufacturing failure at such a time can cause a major corporate setback, and failures are not unusual. As one aerospace executive said when Airbus finally delivered its A380 airplane after significant delays: "Never mind the A380 launch trouble; in the history of aerospace there has never been an on-time and on-quality new model launch. Typically what is launched is too late, is deeply immature, and requires years of fine tuning."

A single employee mistake or one deviation in thousands of standard operating procedures can disable a company, especially when safety-critical consumer products are involved. When you multiply this risk by the fact that the manufacturing workforce is often the largest in a company, with the most exposure to safety hazards, the large potential liabilities inherent in careless operations becomes clearer. Appreciation for manufacturing, as too many companies are learning the hard way after product incidents or safety accidents, is at the very least one of the most effective ways to avoid unnecessary risk.

PROCTER & GAMBLE: MANUFACTURING AS A GROWTH ENGINE

Keith Harrison, P&G's global product supply officer, manages the manufacturing of roughly 300 brands in 145 plants around the world. These products cost approximately $40 billion to make and generate $77 billion in sales. The organization comprises approximately 65,000 P&G employees, and its functions span purchasing, logistics, engineering, manufacturing, quality assurance, and information technology.

What is the status of manufacturing at P&G?
Harrison: Our supply organization is expected to add significant value to our company, and our internal manufacturing capability is core to the success of our supply organization. In my view, supply operations can be growth engines. To make this aspiration real, we have set a target of generating $1 billion of

top-line revenue growth through supply chain operations, and so far we have already verified a potential $800 million.

To name one example, we developed a very
flexible technology that can print each box of Pringles
chips separately in a split second. This allows us to
offer retailers more customized products by making
label changes instantly and on smaller product
batches. In another example, we reduced stock-outs
[in which retailers do not have enough stock to meet
consumer demand] by 50 percent and made demonstrable additional revenues.

Manufacturing, in our mind, is absolutely central
to all of this. If you don't have a manufacturing system and workforce that can deal with the complexity and the changes in your markets and products,
you are lost.

**How much pressure does the demand for prod-
uct variety place on P&G's manufacturing operations?**
Harrison: Over the past years we doubled the number of SKUs in our historical business alone. To deal
with this and our steady organic growth, we have
invested in planning systems and production technology like quick changeover technologies. Very im-
portantly, we have worked with our people in the
plants to embrace the realization that this growth in
complexity is manageable and a sign of strength. I
would not say that they revel in complexity, but now

we all have a much more positive attitude toward the growing number of products that our plants need to produce.

Here, too, we have an example of manufacturing at P&G refusing to be a "passive" function. In the past, manufacturing has had to produce new products and only afterwards has complained that these products carry a huge extra cost burden. Now, we have calculation models that allow us to say, "We can produce that product but it will cost another 15 cents per unit," before we start making it. And for every initiative, we calculate the total delivered cost. In this way, we can have a constructive dialogue with the rest of our company about the fact that manufacturing requires some investment to produce new products. We allow our company to make go/no-go decisions about products before it is too late.

How do you ensure your shop floor communities do not become disenfranchised as in so many other companies?

Harrison: We don't think it's necessary to organize a circus to keep our workforce engaged. We don't typically have to pay huge variable salaries and certainly don't have Starbucks in our plants.

What is important for us is that our plant employees are not caged in by too narrowly defined task packages. We have an initiative called "walk the supply chain" in which our people regularly move between upstream and downstream segments of the manufacturing process. We have a very flexible workforce system, and our people own it. We do typically pay among the best salaries in the industry, and we treat our people very well. Another part of our culture that is very constructive is that we do all we can to avoid fear of failure. Constructive dissatisfaction is important. Finally, we promote from within. If you want to progress, you can, and that includes moving into a position outside of manufacturing.

It is rarer for talent outside manufacturing to move into significant manufacturing roles. But that, too, occurs at P&G. We have a former sales professional who now is a plant manager, and there are other examples. These are not coincidences; P&G's career model requires multidisciplinary, multibusiness, and multigeography experience.

What is P&G's position on outsourcing?
Harrison: In principle, we prefer to keep manufacturing in-house, but only if we can prove that we have a competitive advantage versus contract manufacturers. We regularly benchmark to test our competitiveness, and in the vast majority of cases our manufacturing activities stand that test. We are even in the process of insourcing certain products that turned out to be more expensive to outsource over a longer period of time. This means that senior management now thinks that manufacturing at P&G is a competitive advantage.

How important is the role of production equipment innovation in creating a competitive advantage in manufacturing?

Harrison: We have strategic relationships with about 150 low-cost machine builders, but the core innovation for our manufacturing processes remains in-house. We allocate specific modules of the machine to these low-cost builders, but no one sees the whole picture but us. We are open to innovation from the outside and, in fact, across the entire business we expect about 50 percent of our innovation to come from outside the company. But again, process innovation is a core capability for us, and we maintain mastership over the whole development and construction process.

How far has P&G gone on the lean journey?

Harrison: We have exchanges with Toyota to see how their lean concepts translate to our environment, but that is not always easy. For example, how do you apply takt-time to our high-speed filling lines? We want lean concepts driven by the workforce. So far, we are focusing on Total Production Maintenance and "reliability first." Over time, we plan to build other lean elements into it. In this early stage of lean we put great emphasis on appearance—just the overall cleanliness and orderliness of the place and the sense of ownership and respect of the plant community toward its assets. There is no plant that works well that does not look great and does not have a great safety record.

BEYOND MINDSET TO STRATEGY

An appreciative mindset is only the first step toward manufacturing success. Companies that hope to become competitive must embrace their role as manufacturing leaders, with the continuous expansion of learning and capability as the source of strategic advantage. This is easier said than done. It requires adopting the goal of manufacturing excellence, which, in turn, requires a rigorous examination of a company's current capabilities and comparisons to its competitors. An analysis like this must take into account four dimensions of manufacturing excellence:

➤ *Technological distinctiveness.* In manufacturing parlance, technological distinctiveness comprises the "inherent" factors embodied in the process and product design and the technologies that support them.

➤ *Network sophistication.* Those factors comprising network sophistication, known as the "structural" factors, involve the decisions that drive location, size, and utilization of plants, as well as vertical integration and supply chain organization.

➤ *In-plant transformation.* The "systemic" factors that make up in-plant transformation are related to the way manufacturing is conducted within a plant: the procedures and systems, such as lean processes, sales and operations planning procedures, and the choice and application of IT support systems. All of these help determine quality, efficiency, and performance within a factory.

➤ *Labor modernization.* These "realized" factors of manufacturing have to do with the motivation of people working in manufacturing and the incentives put in place for
them.

By analyzing the costs and potential benefits in each of
these four domains, one can gain an overall and in-depth
picture of a manufacturer's strengths and weaknesses, the
combination of industrial relations and worker motivation, plant processes and systems, plant networks, vertical integration, process and product design, and other
factors that can make a company either a follower or an industry leader in manufacturing. (This is known as the ISSR
diagnostic, named after the inherent, structural, systemic,
and realized dimensions that it delineates.)

The analysis can also become the basis for one's own
manufacturing strategy: which products, processes, and
process technology to invest in and develop; what plants
should be located where; what products they should make;
how to achieve standard work, lean culture, and operating
improvements; and lastly, how to engage the manufacturing workforce.

Recently, a large automotive company used this framework to determine how to improve its competitive position. Its first plan—to install a new lean system and close a
number of assembly lines—had been shelved because of
union protests against the jobs that would have been cut.
The unions countered that the company should embed new
flexible technology in existing lines and leave jobs intact.

In the process of analysis, the company learned that
closing its assembly lines (a structural factor) would

indeed eliminate some costs. Enhancing factory flexibility (an inherent factor) would have a still bigger impact on costs per unit. But there were so many inefficiencies in the plant's processes and procedures (the systemic factors) that these dwarfed the savings available through other means. The analysis proved that closing the cost gap with its primary competitor was impossible without a full-fledged lean program, and the fact-based analytical approach convinced the unions to support the company's turnaround program.

It bears noting that although the ultimate objective of this analysis is excellence in all four dimensions, excellence in just one or two of them can suffice to put a company in an industry-leading position. P&G, for instance, already excels in the inherent technology dimension, is now focused on the structural network dimension, is starting to tackle parts of the systemic dimension, and is not too concerned about the realized drivers. This combination is enough to fend off almost all competitive threats. Toyota excels at the systemic and to a lesser extent at realized levels, but has equally formidable competitors at the inherent (e.g., Honda's manufacturing technologies) and the structural levels.

Choosing when to focus on which dimension depends on the manufacturing economics of the industry and the gaps between current performance and the best possible performance in the various dimensions. Such explicit insights should be the basis for any manufacturing strategy, but they rarely are. In fact, even the more basic forms of performance comparisons in manufacturing are often flawed and misleading. Key performance indicators used to steer manufacturing operations usually focus on the operational level as opposed to the strategic level and are rarely balanced. For example, they measure input cost or output performance, but not both.

More balanced metrics might include "total cost of quality" and "total cost of maintenance" as a percent of plant sales; these would enable comparisons of prevention, appraisal, and quality (rework, scrap, and so forth) across production facilities. But these measures are rarely found in practice.

The analysis can also help savvy manufacturers consider the implementation sequence of their actions. Commonly, companies prioritize improvement actions by the potential reward, ease of implementation, or risk—usually starting with those that are simplest to implement and offer the best immediate rewards. In the end, however, overall success rates depend on a more deliberate sequence. For example, a plant consolidation followed by the rollout of an in-plant excellence program requires a careful analysis of capabilities and labor relations within the redundant factories. The excellence program should follow the generic rule of first fixing the basics using techniques such as 5S and visual management, then stabilizing operations by creating standard operations and improving takt time, and only then approaching excellence with the help of pull scheduling and systems installation.

The ISSR approach is comprehensive; it puts the four major dimensions of manufacturing excellence into a common context. Each of these dimensions, in turn, comprises its own set of basic prescriptions. In the next four sections, we will examine how each of these dimensions can yield both short-term gains and long-term advantage.

INSIDE AN ISSR ANALYSIS

What does an ISSR analysis look like? How does a company use it to reveal why competitors enjoy advantage, or to set priorities? The answer begins with the data. Costs and potential performance gains are analyzed for each of the four performance drivers: technological distinctiveness ("inherent"), network sophistication ("structural"), in-plant transformation ("systemic"), and labor modernization ("realized"). For each set of drivers, as shown in Exhibit 4-1, there are subdrivers; as these are changed or improved, the costs in each part of the system can be reduced. Inherent and structural factors are largely determined by corporate and manufacturing strategy;

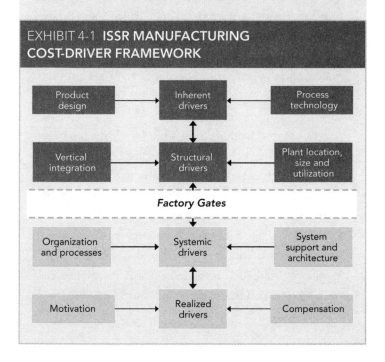

EXHIBIT 4-1 **ISSR MANUFACTURING COST-DRIVER FRAMEWORK**

systemic and realized factors are determined by factory-based manufacturing tactics and operational execution.

By providing visibility into the factors that influence performance in manufacturing operations, and by enabling direct comparisons among plants (or companies), ISSR supports the establishment and pursuit of realistic performance targets. Confronted with price competition, for example, a manufacturer can use ISSR to determine how far it—or its competitors—can reduce prices without seriously compromising financial health.

An ISSR analysis can thus replace the suboptimal ways that many companies set objectives: the arbitrary targets that are imposed from above on so many plants; the benchmarks which rarely take into account all critical factors that vary widely between plants; and the bottom-up operational reviews, which are labor intensive and lack insights into competitors.

The waterfall chart in Exhibit 4-2 illustrates how the ISSR framework identifies cost reduction opportunities. Each category shows how one's own plant (the black bar at the top) might change to match the operational advantages and disadvantages of the competitor's plant (the black bar at the bottom). By identifying the impact in terms of cost per unit performance, manufacturers can begin to answer essential and detailed questions: How much will the cost gap grow if a competitor installs a specific technology? Or how much will the gap grow if the competitor increases its plant utilization by 30 percent? As a company explores its options by considering various "what-if" scenarios, the shape of the "waterfall" shifts, showing the relative advantage or disadvantage of various strategic options.

EXHIBIT 4-2 ISSR: COMPARISON OF COST STRUCTURES OF A GERMAN AND A ROMANIAN ASSEMBLY PLANT

Correction for	Cost Structure	
	Reference	100%
• Labor costs • Premium/shift deltas • Annual work hours • Productivity	If Reference produced at the same location as the competitor	-26.7% — Realized Difference
		73.3%
• Indirect + overhead ratios • Organizational differences • Maintenance intensity • IT costs	If Reference also had the same management and support systems	-2.6% — Systemic Difference
		70.7%
• Scale effects • Utilization effects • Complexity effects • Scope impact	If Reference also had the same structures as the competitor	15.4% — Structural Difference
		86.1%
• Choice of technology • Product design	If Reference produced exactly as the competitor does	-6.2% — Inherent Difference
	Competition	79.8%

Source: Booz Allen Hamilton Analysis

The First Driver: Technological Distinctiveness

Until very recently, investment in the design and engineering of manufacturing technologies was a choice rather than a necessity. But that is changing. Equipment innovation has become one of the most effective ways to counter the challenges imposed by product variety, material shortages, and labor shortages and conflict. Indeed, done well, new production technologies can address many of manufacturing's greatest challenges simultaneously.

Unfortunately, over the past several decades, many manufacturers have lost their edge in technological and process innovation. Instead, they have relied on machine builders and other vendors to fill the gap. This has not worked well: equipment manufacturers do not generally have a strong track record for innovation, particularly for the kinds of creative and customized breakthroughs that would allow their client companies to leapfrog past competitors. Even when machine builders offer an innovative new technology, its competitive advantage for any company is negated by its availability on the open market.

Another reason that process innovation capabilities have languished is the investment in time, capital, and executive attention that they require. As a general rule of thumb, it can take two or more years for a capital investment in process innovation to bear fruit in the semiconductor sector, five or more years in assembly manufacturing, and 10 or more years in certain process industries, such as the chemicals industry. Additionally, to implement these upgrades, companies must disrupt ongoing operations and train entire plant communities to use different tools and techniques, and to adopt fresh ways of working.

Sometimes, a promising process innovation effort is disbanded because top management changes or because the sponsoring executives lose interest. Outmoded techniques and practices can endure for decades in some companies, as they cycle through a series of half-realized quality-improvement or plant-restructuring initiatives. In other companies, process innovations flourish only in the margins of individual plants or uninfluential outposts, never gaining the scale needed to become full-fledged competitive advantages. For example, Nobel Industries (now Akzo Nobel) maintained a coating operations plant in urban Copenhagen. Because of constant economic and environmental pressures, the plant developed a number of low-cost, high-intelligence process enhancements. But Nobel was never able to transfer them throughout the broader enterprise and thus did not capture their full potential.

The investment in process technology also varies widely between nations. There is an obvious deficit in the United States, where many plants suffer from lack of automation, overreliance on vendors for process technology, inadequately educated and trained manufacturing engineers, outdated equipment, and atrophying skills. One U.S. auto parts plant was forced to mothball a brand new automated line imported from one of the company's own European plants because it lacked the know-how and scale to use it. Fifty feet away from the abandoned equipment, assembly workers did the same work manually.

In contrast, in Japan, advances and investments in manufacturing technology and processes are highly respected and avidly pursued. At Toyota and Honda, with the strong support of top management, process technology advances are developed in-house, where a constant array of new ideas are in the design and test phases. One result: Honda is spending *less* on its flexible and automated manufacturing technology than its U.S. and European competitors pony up for their outmoded systems, yet Honda's body shops can assemble eight very different models each, versus fewer similar models in most other automakers' shops.

Manufacturing companies can take three major steps to capture the gains inherent in technological distinctiveness:

First and most obvious, they must understand the value of process innovation and invest in it. We estimate that measured against sales, the most successful manufacturers—companies like Toyota, Procter & Gamble, and Lego—spend more than twice as much on process innovation per sales dollar as other firms in their industries.

Second, they must establish a central home for process technology development, with visibility and influence throughout the company. The successful manufacturer of the future will have its engineers overseeing process and equipment innovation for the entire organization, rather than running from factory to factory, doing day-to-day troubleshooting. Manufacturing engineers should be focused on planning strategic improvements; for example, they should have the financial skills required to make compelling business cases for innovation investments.

In elevating manufacturing engineers to a more centralized, strategic role, companies will also come closer to reaping the promised benefits of the design for manufacturing (DFM) and design to cost (DTC) concepts. DFM, which emerged in the late 1980s, seeks to unite R&D, engineering, and manufacturing in such initiatives as parts standardization and improving manufacturing efficiency through product redesign. But the concept has yet to attain its full potential. The costs of this lapse can be significant: at one equipment maker, the cost of using nonstandardized parts in its different products totaled a full 15 percent of its overall manufacturing costs.

The development of DFM and DTC has been hampered by prioritization and expense of engineering time. But with the growing base of engineers in Asia and Eastern Europe and the steady outsourcing of manufacturing engineering tasks to those countries, a revitalization of both DFM and DTC is already in the works in some industries, such as aerospace, and seems likely to spread.

AN ENGINEERING TALENT CRUNCH

Recently, one major automaker found that to meet process development needs over the next few decades, it would have to nearly double its engineering man-hours. This was a daunting prospect because engineers were in short supply and hiring them involved personnel searches that would take up to nine months.

At the same time, the automaker discovered that it was not using its current engineering talent to its full potential. In fact, 78 percent of its engineers were assigned to its plants versus an ideal of about 35 percent. This diffusion of engineering firepower created two problems. The first was wasted talent: at least 40 percent of the engineers' time spent was in routine trouble-shooting, so-called babysitting tasks that could just as easily be handled by the operations staff. The second was skill loss: as they relegated themselves to housekeeping tasks, the engineers' know-how was evaporating from lack of use.

Third, manufacturers must reclaim many of the process technology development activities that have been ceded to equipment suppliers. This will force them to relearn skills that can be applied to all aspects of manufacturing technology design, development, purchase, and implementation.

Rebuilding their process technology capabilities will help manufacturers be better informed purchasers of new equipment and more expeditious implementers. One automaker recently attempted to put in place an extremely advanced cooperative robotics system in which one robot welds a part as another robot carries it. The system failed to work because the company didn't realize at first the intensive programming skill needed to operate it; this in turn caused a delay in the launch of a critical new car.

Skillful manufacturers often become codesigners with their process equipment suppliers. For example, Toyota recently jointly pioneered a new mechanical press with its supplier Komatsu; the new system boasts faster cycle times, better dimensional tolerances, and lower die costs. The project took advantage of Toyota's know-how in manufacturing systems, Komatsu's in equipment design, and both companies' know-how in process technology. Toyota is the first major auto manufacturer to have it, likely giving it a competitive advantage for a specified period of time, after which Komatsu will be able to market the product more broadly.

Process technology capabilities will become increasingly important as flexible manufacturing continues to become more prevalent, and as competition compels companies to provide expanded variety at ever lower cost. Consider, once again, the automotive industry, where manufacturing flexibility is already becoming a make-or-break factor. Automakers are expanding their lineups of both chassis platforms and models. Some, like Toyota and Honda, are restricting options but are producing more platforms on each manufacturing line. Others, such as the German manufacturers, are betting they can build relatively inexpensive, but highly customized cars. In both cases, flexible manufacturing equipment will be a major key to their success. In addition, flexibility should ultimately help manufacturers ameliorate the costs of short product life cycles; the same production systems can be reused with minor tinkering for new products.

MODEL FLEXIBILITY FOR CARMAKERS

Although flexibility is not an appropriate strategy for every market, plant, product, or process technology (mainly because of the implementation costs), it is already an essential capability in many sectors. This includes the automotive industry, where high capital costs, difficulties of predicting demand, and labor costs that are often fixed by union agreements combine to make manufacturing flexibility a valuable trait.

There are two primary dimensions of flexibility in auto manufacturing. *Network flexibility* seeks to optimize vehicle output by moving production among factories and locations according to demand. *Model flexibility* seeks to expand the capabilities of assembly lines so that they accommodate more products or product variants, as well as optimal product mixes and volumes. (An offshoot of the latter is *generation flexibility*, which seeks to reduce the expenses and time related to the switching over of lines to accommodate new models of existing products.)

One primary goal of model flexibility is to increase operating margin and decrease capital costs. Among automakers, model changeovers often cost hundreds of millions of dollars and involve the construction of entirely new body shops and extensive equipment upgrades. To reduce this cost, leading automakers are starting to think ahead; they are building today's processes to accommodate tomorrow's cars without altering the lion's share of their equipment, systems, and technology. Model flexibility also enables companies to improve their revenues by producing more differentiated models while keeping plant volumes and utilization high. Finally, model flexibility can also help automotive companies produce fewer cars when demand is low. When the market becomes flooded with a particular vehicle, resale values drop and new prices follow used prices, often for the entire brand. In environments like this, the ability to judiciously regulate production speed can have a substantial impact on near-term and long-term pricing of a model and a brand.

Model flexibility requires innovative engineering and very clear design parameters for new cars, but some automakers are achieving it. Toyota, for instance, has achieved model flexibility with its global body line (GBL), which combines a relatively standard body shop template and manual processes that eliminate the costly retooling and reprogramming of robotics when new models are launched. The company also reengineered its main assembly line from a multitooling to a single-tooling system; now jigs can be adjusted to the dimensions of different models almost seamlessly. In addition, Toyota has created ancillary work cells dedicated to select, highly differentiated model components while maintaining fixed cells on the primary body lines. The result: GBL has reduced Toyota capital expenses in its body shops–related new vehicle launches by as much as 70 percent.

Because it can be a challenge to maintain quality when workers must make rapid and complex decisions about when and how to install components and parts in various products, Toyota created its "set parts system" (SPS). In SPS, subsystems are built separately and delivered to the line in proper assembly sequence. This eliminates decisions, as line workers simply bolt each subsystem into the vehicle at hand. SPS has shortened final assembly lines by 50 percent, and Toyota has reduced net labor requirements by

10 to 15 percent, while simultaneously reducing task complexity and meeting high quality standards.

Honda, too, has built flexibility into its factories. It is using strict, repeating design parameters between models, so that standardized work cells are able to produce increasing numbers of subassemblies and body lines for many different car models. To accomplish this, the company employs a "batch" process, enabling the robotic system to swap tools for different models during changeovers and generating a greater variety of product in the same area. Honda's batch approach also clarifies assembly part choices despite the added complexity of running numerous models down a single line.

Unlike Toyota, which sequences incoming parts, Honda has installed part racks dedicated to specific models on its lines. Honda is reaping benefits from its batch-production-based flexibility. Recently, the company effortlessly and inexpensively added the Civic to its existing Alliston, Ontario, plant to meet soaring demand for a new model of the high-mileage car. (In this case, model flexibility and network flexibility worked hand in hand.)

Flexibility is also valuable in lower-volume auto plants. BMW, for instance, has enhanced flexibility by reducing body variants and then producing multiple models in a single plant. BMW currently is producing the Z4 two-seater, the X5 SUV, and the new X6 on the same line. This has helped it maintain high output levels in all of its plants and avoid the subscale inefficiencies associated with low volumes.

Though model flexibility can be extremely advantageous, there are occasions when producing multiple brands on the same line is not economically sound or strategically essential. Typically, this is the case for hugely popular products, such as the Toyota Camry. About 400,000 Camrys are sold each year in the United States, and Toyota's Georgetown, Kentucky, plant hums along at virtually full capacity to meet the demand. Adding the cost and complexity of multiple models to a line like this would reduce profitability and not be optimal.

Model flexibility may also be unnecessary when there is little or no product customization. Indian conglomerate Tata Motors, for instance, is releasing a $2,500 car in 2008. This product is intended to be high volume—more than 350,000 vehicles annually. There will be virtually no custom options available in the car, a strategy that will enable the company to avoid all of the expenses associated with model flexibility and keep the price low enough to attract the massive customer base in its home market, as well as developing countries around the world.

Process innovation can also help solve the workforce shortages and labor conflicts that challenge so many manufacturers. At the far end of the spectrum is the "lights-out factory" (named for the idea that, with minimal human labor, there would be no need for visual illumination). This could presumably solve many workforce challenges, but it has yet to be realized in batch and discrete manufacturing. In more practical terms, there is still a huge opportunity to be gained in replacing a myriad of manual and sometimes risky tasks with simple, often off-the-shelf automation solutions. In the average automotive or aerospace parts plant, it is not unusual to find surface treatment and painting departments where workers manually place thousands of parts on trays, paint them, turn them, and paint them once more. In the average food or batch chemicals plant, it isn't unusual to find workers manually loading and unloading reactors and vessels. The industrial world is full of unrealized automation opportunities that could be captured with a bit more attention from the engineering staff and a better-lubricated investment approval process.

The Second Driver: Network Sophistication

Most companies organize the global setup of their production and supply operations on a project-by-project basis. When competitive conditions change or when top-down financial demands require it, they react in piecemeal fashion, moving a plant from Indiana to Mexico, or from Mexico to Vietnam. In doing so, they miss the opportunities embedded in viewing plant networks as flexible, integrated supply chains that can be reconfigured as needed anywhere in the world.

It is striking how few companies continuously and proactively analyze their manufacturing network in terms of a single global footprint. This oversight leads to any number of missteps; perhaps the most common is underestimating the impact of scale and utilization. A company might offshore half of the production of an older Western plant to a plant in a low-cost nation, only to find that it has unintentionally destroyed the older plant's economic basis by relegating its high fixed costs and expensive technical capabilities to less volume. Meanwhile, the factory in the low-cost nation underperforms too, because it lacks the volume needed to attract a supply base and cover its overhead.

Network sophistication requires a more enlightened and agile approach to manufacturing footprints, a flexible approach that can create tremendous advantages. It can take years to close down and move a factory (typically after several years of wavering over the decision to shutter it in the first place), but it should only take months or weeks to shift production or reconfigure plants within a flexible network.

Such flexible networks are still relatively rare, but they are being used with great success in a few dozen large organizations. Among them: The U.S. Army, which constantly and proactively reassigns military bases and their supply operations to fresh uses. Another is a European manufacturer of specialized air conditioning supplies which, in one far-reaching and novel implementation, built its factories on large freighters that move from port to port between the southern and northern hemispheres as the seasonal marketplace changes. The company has not publicized this innovative approach, rightly perceiving it as a competitive advantage, but it is already being copied. Cement International in Qatar has built a cement factory on a ship, which docks wherever in the Persian Gulf its products are needed.

Driven by rising transportation costs, lower capital costs, and growing market uncertainty, a number of companies, mainly in consumer goods and building materials, are creating sophisticated networks. As a result, instead of building megaplants (as Warner Lambert did in the late 1990s when it tried to consolidate Listerine production into just one plant worldwide), these companies are moving toward more distributed networks that provide the lowest fixed cost. One leading consumer goods company is particularly interested in creating such a network, intending thus to safeguard its long-term commitments to its existing manufacturing plants and their surrounding communities. The new setup would allow it to right-size plants painlessly enough to maintain healthy plants anywhere.

The desired characteristics of networks that support such goals typically include:

➤ Globally standardized manufacturing lines that are at the leading edge of technology in terms of output per hour, lowest man-hour requirements, etc.

➤ Modular lines that can be easily disassembled and rebuilt elsewhere by the production workforce

➤ Minimal overhead and indirect costs per manufacturing line, achieved, for example, through the centralization of plant support functions such as planning

➤ Extreme workforce flexibility, including the ability to downsize or increase the workforce, often using high-skilled, leased personnel, by as much as 35 percent

In the future, it is likely that network sophistication will increasingly extend to joint ventures and shared supply chain agreements with other companies, including competitors. In the chemicals and automotive industries, companies are already teaming up with their suppliers to make network decisions together, a stratagem that has helped to reduce supply snafus in newly established plants. But such initiatives are still restricted to those firms that have built a cooperative structure of tiered suppliers, who all feel a stake in one another's success.

In situations where product and process technologies are mature and innovation is a minor factor, one way to manage global network issues is by pooling or swapping capacity with competitors' factories. Today such arrangements are rare, but they do exist, in the outdoor equipment and basic chemicals industries, for example. Despite the risks, the benefits are clear: increasing factory footprints can enable manufacturers to better optimize plant utilization and improve cost structures, especially with regard to transportation.

Defining where to position what capacity is one obvious aspect of network sophistication. Another less obvious aspect is determining the proper degree of vertical integration: how much direct participation in the various manufacturing steps from raw materials to finished goods is appropriate. To identify the optimum level of vertical integration, companies must differentiate their manufacturing activities and determine how to best maximize their networks for each different facet of the production sequence. Every industry has a distinct set of variables to analyze in this regard. For example, in the metalworking industry, a company might choose to break its production activities down into substeps: cutting, forming, connecting, preassembly, and assembly. Each substep would have its own place in the manufacturing network; some might be outsourced, some might be shared with other companies, others might be located flexibly, and still others might be closely managed in a very few specific plants.

Claas, the German agricultural equipment maker introduced in Chapter 3, has demonstrated the value that can be unlocked when the right network formula of geographical sites and vertical integration is found. In the midst of substantial competitive pressure and as part of a constant drive to improve efficiency, the company carefully selected manufacturing steps for outsourcing—starting all the way upstream with metal-cutting processes and gradually rolling up more downstream activities, all the while focusing internal excellence on preassembly and assembly activities. In a creative move, Claas spun off one downstream factory through a management buyout and transformed it into a primary supplier. The newly formed supplier signed up additional customers, using the added volume and reengineered processes to raise its quality standards and better balance capacity. The improvements also enhanced employee motivation. Today, the plant's revitalization stands in stark contrast to much of the region's slumping commodity, machining, and metalworking factories.

FINDING THE OPTIMAL FOOTPRINT

As one global automotive supplier of complex parts for engines recently discovered, finding the optimal manufacturing footprint requires sound strategic thinking and solid analytics. This company had three plants: two in Europe, servicing the majority of the

EXHIBIT 4-3 **COST SCALE CURVE IN DIFFERENT COUNTRIES**

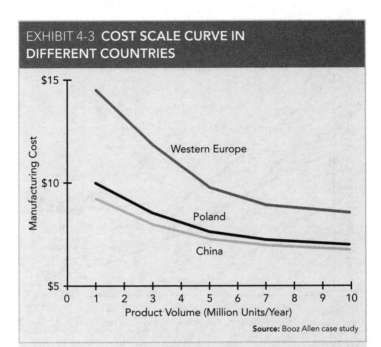

Source: Booz Allen case study

regional demand for its products, and one in the United States. It wanted to determine:

➤ The footprint that would offer the lowest-cost, highest-quality production

➤ The impact on costs of the structure and technology in its brownfield sites (established factories with long-standing workforces)

➤ Its competitive exposure and how best to protect itself

To find these answers, the supplier first calculated and compared cost scale curves based on volume in three plants in different nations (Exhibit 4-3). It discovered that raising volume from 1.25 million

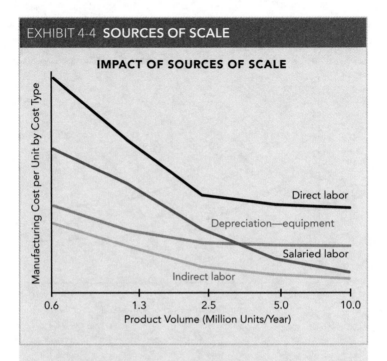

EXHIBIT 4-4 **SOURCES OF SCALE**

IMPACT OF SOURCES OF SCALE

Manufacturing Cost per Unit by Cost Type

Direct labor

Depreciation—equipment

Salaried labor

Indirect labor

Product Volume (Million Units/Year)

0.6   1.3   2.5   5.0   10.0

units per year to 5 million units per year in its existing plant in Western Europe would lower its cost per unit by 25 percent, but that the same increase in volume would cost nearly $2 per unit less in a Chinese factory.

In analyzing the source of the volume savings, the supplier further found the greatest benefit derived from reduced direct labor costs (Exhibit 4-4). This suggested that more and more advanced process technology and automation could be cost-effectively implemented as volume increased, enabling a significant decrease in direct labor costs.

Next, the supplier analyzed the delivered cost of

its product from various locations (Exhibit 4-5). It found that a 1.25 million unit volume in the West Europe plant had a 29 percent unit cost disadvantage compared to a similar plant in China, and that as volume grew to 5 million units, the disadvantage *increased* to 38 percent. However, because of the reduced logistics expense and cost of transportation to Western markets, at 5 million units, factories in the lower-cost European nations of Poland and Czechoslovakia offered at least the same per unit rates as factories in China.

Finally, the supplier analyzed the cost structure of each of its competitors based on their process technology, the wage rates of their locations, the scale of their facilities, and other data. It found that it faced one large and dangerous Western European rival (Competitor 1), which produced twice its volume with lower costs, a number of smaller competitors (on the upper side of Exhibit 4-6) with insufficient scale and excessive production costs, and one Chinese rival (at the bottom) with lower costs, but less volume.

Based on these findings, the company realized that it needed to create a more defensible manufacturing footprint. It analyzed its options and decided to consolidate production into two low-cost country facilities (one in Eastern Europe serving the European market; one in China serving the rest of the world) to achieve the best balance of scale and per unit cost. Moreover, the supplier identified new

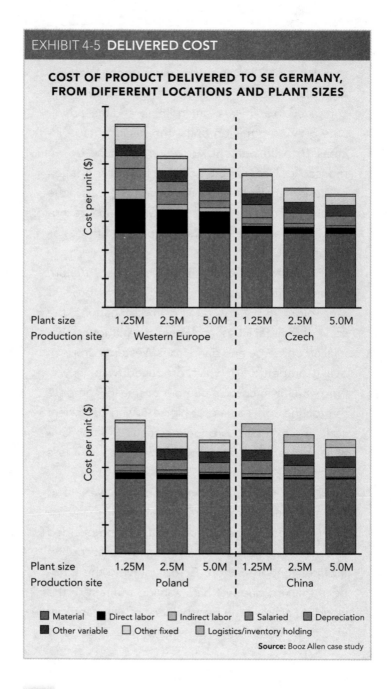

EXHIBIT 4-5 **DELIVERED COST**

COST OF PRODUCT DELIVERED TO SE GERMANY, FROM DIFFERENT LOCATIONS AND PLANT SIZES

Cost per unit ($)

| Plant size | 1.25M | 2.5M | 5.0M | 1.25M | 2.5M | 5.0M |
| Production site | | Western Europe | | | Czech | |

Cost per unit ($)

| Plant size | 1.25M | 2.5M | 5.0M | 1.25M | 2.5M | 5.0M |
| Production site | | Poland | | | China | |

■ Material ■ Direct labor ☐ Indirect labor ■ Salaried ■ Depreciation
■ Other variable ☐ Other fixed ☐ Logistics/inventory holding

Source: Booz Allen case study

EXHIBIT 4-6 COST COMPARISONS IN PRACTICE

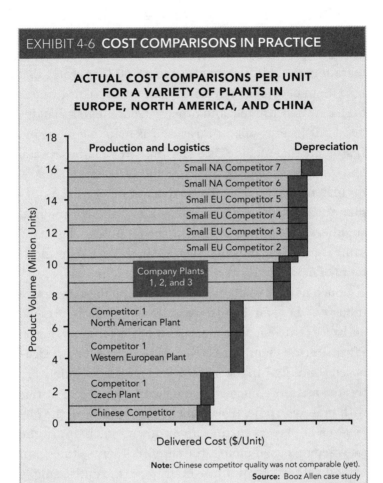

**ACTUAL COST COMPARISONS PER UNIT
FOR A VARIETY OF PLANTS IN
EUROPE, NORTH AMERICA, AND CHINA**

Production and Logistics — Depreciation

Product Volume (Million Units) — Delivered Cost ($/Unit)

- Small NA Competitor 7
- Small NA Competitor 6
- Small EU Competitor 5
- Small EU Competitor 4
- Small EU Competitor 3
- Small EU Competitor 2
- Company Plants 1, 2, and 3
- Competitor 1 North American Plant
- Competitor 1 Western European Plant
- Competitor 1 Czech Plant
- Chinese Competitor

Note: Chinese competitor quality was not comparable (yet).
Source: Booz Allen case study

process technologies that would help it achieve lower costs at lower volumes than its primary competitor. Although the supplier is still in the process of implementing its new footprint, it expects that this plan will deliver in excess of $150 million in net present value.

As plant networks expand and change more frequently, and as companies create new constellations of vertical integration, the ability to manage the supplier networks that feed them becomes increasingly important. This trend is fueled by new product and process technologies that depend on closer cooperation as well as manufacturing investments that include risk-sharing agreements between end-producers and suppliers. In the aerospace industry, for instance, Boeing has divested major sections of its airplane manufacturing to smaller, more entrepreneurial suppliers and some newly established suppliers, but at the same time it demands that each co-invest in the development of new composite manufacturing technologies.

Such new constellations bring to mind the automotive industry, where for decades two different supply base models have coexisted: our colleagues Bill Jackson and Michael Pfitzmann call them "price-based sourcing" and "knowledge-based sourcing." In the price-based model, suppliers are treated as interchangeable and clearly separate entities with their own objectives, which often clash with the objectives of players further up or down the chain. In the knowledge-based model, the suppliers across the chain work together to grow the overall "pie" (the entire supply chain), confident that if they do, their slice will get bigger. Technology is jointly developed and shared. Production plans are shared, too, and lean, just-in-time deliveries are the rule rather than the exception.

As illustrated in Exhibit 4-7, the price-based model closely resembles the actual state of affairs at most Western car makers; the knowledge-based model is a desired end-state which was pioneered and continues to be

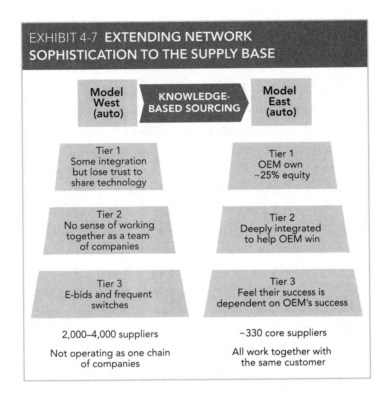

EXHIBIT 4-7 **EXTENDING NETWORK SOPHISTICATION TO THE SUPPLY BASE**

Model West (auto)	KNOWLEDGE-BASED SOURCING	Model East (auto)
Tier 1 Some integration but lose trust to share technology		Tier 1 OEM own ~25% equity
Tier 2 No sense of working together as a team of companies		Tier 2 Deeply integrated to help OEM win
Tier 3 E-bids and frequent switches		Tier 3 Feel their success is dependent on OEM's success
2,000–4,000 suppliers		~330 core suppliers
Not operating as one chain of companies		All work together with the same customer

approached by a handful of Asian companies. Given tomorrow's manufacturing challenges, the knowledge-based model is an appealing alternative, and not just in the auto industry. However, time has shown that breaking out of the price-based model requires decisive action and a long-term commitment. It often involves supplier consolidation, a culture shift within the purchasing and manufacturing functions, a new set of metrics that enable a comprehensive view of cost, and a very different set of trade-offs for the manufacturer of the ultimate branded product.

The Third Driver: In-Plant Transformation

It is now more than 30 years since the notion of manufacturing excellence—variously attributed to the Toyota production system, sociotechnical systems, total quality management, lean manufacturing, and high-performance systems—was introduced to factories worldwide. But plants that have successfully achieved efficient and optimal operations are still few and far between. Thus, the potential competitive advantage in shop floor transformation and optimization remains as high as the barriers to success.

The typical performance gaps between the average automotive plant and truly lean operations are illustrated in Exhibit 4-8, which reveals that the potential for performance improvement implied by true leanness is enormous, particularly with regard to quality, inventory, and productivity gains. Even the smaller performance gaps for launch and delivery reliability are significant. These two measures are customer facing, and one percentage point of slippage can have dramatic repercussions on revenues. Moreover, these dimensions of performance improvement tend to be interrelated; pushing hard on just one of them can create other inefficiencies. One aerospace manufacturer, for example, met its delivery date by shipping unfinished components—along with the technicians needed to complete them—to its customers' assembly lines.

The difficulty of transforming brownfield sites to process-savvy showcases is illustrated by the slow progress that many companies make in the quest to adopt lean production. In the aerospace industry, for example, both

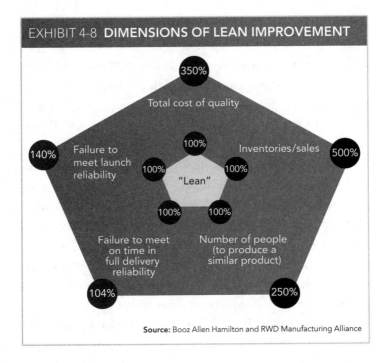

EXHIBIT 4-8 **DIMENSIONS OF LEAN IMPROVEMENT**

350%

Total cost of quality

140%

Failure to meet launch reliability

100%

Inventories/sales

500%

100%

100%

"Lean"

100%

100%

Failure to meet on time in full delivery reliability

Number of people (to produce a similar product)

104%

250%

Source: Booz Allen Hamilton and RWD Manufacturing Alliance

Boeing and Airbus have made several attempts at lean transformation in the past 15 years. Each time, they seem to learn from their previous efforts. In the automotive industry, virtually every Western company has undertaken lean efforts that have gone through constant starts, stops, and rebrandings.

Why has in-plant transformation lagged when its promise is so compelling? In many companies, the manufacturing community cannot even easily agree upon a lean vision and its components. When they do, lean is often defined in simplistic and generic terms, such as eliminating waste, creating more efficient and better performing flows from input to output in factories, and shifting the organization's culture toward continuous improvement. But lean is not this simple: comprehensive and deeper definitions may involve hundreds of specific criteria.

Next, the adoption and implementation of the lean philosophy is too often treated as a "just do it" initiative—the business and responsibility of plant managers alone. As a result, senior management is never truly engaged in the effort. Lacking that support, the plant managers feel undue pressure to deliver results long before the basis for change is complete. As Tom Burke, chief operating officer of thermal products manufacturer Modine Manufacturing Company, says, "Most companies I have seen want lean results first and only then lean processes, while really lean results only come after a long period of sustained lean behavior." Formulaic objectives also can hinder lean transformations. For instance, it's not uncommon for a factory manager to be directed to reduce labor costs across the board by 10 percent while improving output and quality by 20 percent near term. These objectives may sound reasonable on the surface, but they often prove to be incompatible with each other.

Also, the critical need for standards is often ignored in flawed lean initiatives. True lean operators like to add "waste of the brain" to the "seven wastes" of manufacturing originally articulated by Toyota's Taiichi Ohno. Defining and adhering to standard operating procedures prevents this eighth waste. Only if standards are maintained across the operations can continuous improvement be effectively and efficiently pursued. But the majority of Western manufacturing companies lack work standards across and within their plants, and this is a critical weakness. Professor Shoji Shiba may have predicted this more than 20 years ago. He said that one strength of the Western mind-set would be a major weakness in its quest for manufacturing excellence, namely the sense of intellectual freedom that leads an average employee to continuously challenge the ideas of others. Such common statements as "prove it to me," "I already know it," and "not invented here" indicate attitudes that make it harder to maintain consistent standards.

It is easy to spot lean transformation programs in Fortune 500 companies that have little or no chance of success. Companywide lean programs tend not to succeed when one or more of the following conditions exist:

➤ The program's most engaged champion is a manufacturing manager with little strategic influence on the rest of the organization.

➤ They are overly confined to the supply chain or within the manufacturing function; little concern is given to breaking through the barriers to either engineering or the commercial side of the business.

➤ They are staffed with only a handful of dedicated lean specialists.

➤ They do not have a budget to support the required operating expenses and capital investment.

➤ They project a full and immediate payoff in fewer than two years.

Systemic transformations that fit this description are underpowered, underfunded, poorly planned, and generally unrealistic. Such programs have been described by Jim Parish and Simon Castleman, our colleagues at lean implementation boutique RWD Technologies, as "popcorn lean"; they make noise but don't leave lasting nourishment.

Some major short-term improvements, such as fixing the cost structure and resolving overstaffing, tend to be prerequisites of lean success, especially in brownfields. Installing "intelligent tools," "lean solutions," or "high-performance systems" will not resolve an unsustainable cost structure. If there are more workers than work to do, improving throughput or cycle time speed will not lead to greater bottom-line productivity. In fact, overstaffing decreases the chances of successful lean implementations, in part because overcapacity breeds "process creep," in which workers and managers merely overlay the new lean work rules and practices on top of their old routines. Slimmed-down organizations are much better positioned to perform the right lean moves.

Even when in-plant transformations are properly set up, getting systemic change right remains a tricky business. Successful lean programs use three basic components to achieve their full potential and deliver sustainable results: lean tools, such as *kanban*; lean facilities, such as U-shaped cells; and, most critically, lean cultures. It is the final component—culture—that makes lean transformation efforts so difficult.

Lean programs can deliver short-term results without a cultural transformation, but they never reach their full potential and eventually subside. Full and sustained lean results need a culture supported by vision, skills, incentives, resources, and action plans. This requires:

➤ Effective, committed leadership on the part of a company's most senior executives to create and implant a lean vision.

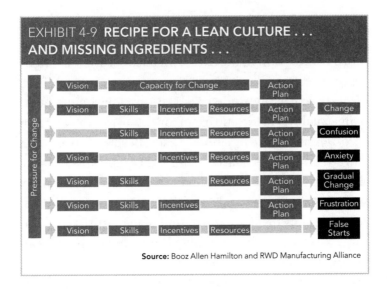

EXHIBIT 4-9 **RECIPE FOR A LEAN CULTURE . . . AND MISSING INGREDIENTS . . .**

Source: Booz Allen Hamilton and RWD Manufacturing Alliance

➤ Capable teams that are selected, developed, and armed with lean skills.

➤ Incentives that support "ownership" of manufacturing transformation (workers recognize they will benefit directly from gains and hold themselves accountable for success) and encourage a self-directed workforce.

➤ Resources, both in adequate labor and financial support.

➤ The forging and execution of a detailed, intelligent action plan.

   If any of the five elements supporting lean cultures are missing, the transformation will end in confusion, anxiety, gradual change, frustration, and false starts—or a mix of these (see Exhibit 4-9).

The successful development of a lean culture invariably starts at the top of the list in Exhibit 4-9 and works down from vision to the skills, incentives, and resources that create the capacity for change to the action plan. These efforts are usually guided and led by policy deployment teams made up of a group of senior executives drawn from across organization functions. Lastly, the creation of a lean culture must be measured. Companies typically measure their performance results and sometimes measure their processes, but very rarely do they measure their cultures. In short, they measure the output of lean initiatives, but forget to measure the key input—the extent to which a lean culture is in place. This measurement can be done in several ways: observing people at work, surveying employees and managers, and tracking key processes in areas such as quality improvement.

One way to think about the lean manufacturing implementation in a plant or a plant network is by comparing it to a computer. Computers depend upon an operating system, the software that coordinates all activity. Manufacturing plants, similarly, require an operating system—a framework of processes, standards, and methodologies that coordinate and set standards for production planning, quality, materials management, and so on. The operating system delineates how performance targets, measurements, and incentives will be set, and provides guidelines for achieving standardized work and continuous improvement initiatives. It also enables performance comparison across similar plants and processes. Finally, it incorporates the behavioral changes required to achieve the manufacturing vision and establishes the manufacturing organization structure, decision points, and conflict reso-lution mechanisms.

Most factory operating systems are ad hoc and rela-tively arbitrary; they have emerged either through trial and error over the course of a plant's history or as copies of sys-tems used in other companies or recommended in text-books. In short, they are generic, not specifically designed with regard to the particular production processes needed by the company in that locale. In-plant transformation, such as adopting lean production, requires consciously re-thinking such operating systems: the way that people and equipment work together. An operating system that is properly planned, addressing both industry dynamics and production processes, and implemented enables a com-pany to accelerate the rate of quality improvement and cost reduction and execute changes in its factory footprint more efficiently.

The best manufacturing operating systems become catalysts for improvement: roadmaps for reorganizing the manufacturing function. In redesigning them, people think freshly about such factors as product development requirements (particularly in the coordination of new de-signs) and ways of training people in new skills. The op-erating systems also specify "line of sight" accountability. This includes the assignment of specific responsibilities to the manufacturing chief, manufacturing directors, plant managers, and supervisors, as well as a feedback loop that tracks how well each member of the management team executes the plan. Finally, the operating systems are flexible enough to facilitate experimentation and change as new ideas emerge.

There are several companies in the auto supplier space that understand the value of a formalized production system. After having tried various approaches to establishing such systems over the years, they are now trying to define a combination of a comprehensive manufacturing vision and extremely specific standard processes, procedures, key performance indicators, and organizational structures in an effort that genuinely involves all plants.

A LEAN ASSESSMENT

Implementing the types of systemic and behavioral changes needed to create a lean factory or factory network begins with a thorough understanding of the existing culture and modes of work. This implies conducting objective assessments that measure the relative readiness and existing support for a lean system within a plant and unearthing the main levers for improvement over the long term. To realistically pinpoint systemic strengths and weaknesses, the diagnostic must be fact-based, that is, it cannot be built on hearsay or surface observation.

The assessments used by our firm in collaboration with RWD, for example, rate the readiness level of plants on a scale of one to five by comparing their operations to a set of fixed expectations. A plant is evaluated on eight separate dimensions featuring 33 key elements. These elements are defined by up to 550 underlying criteria (see Exhibit 4-10).

At their best, lean assessments are comprehensive, rigorous, collaborative processes in which a

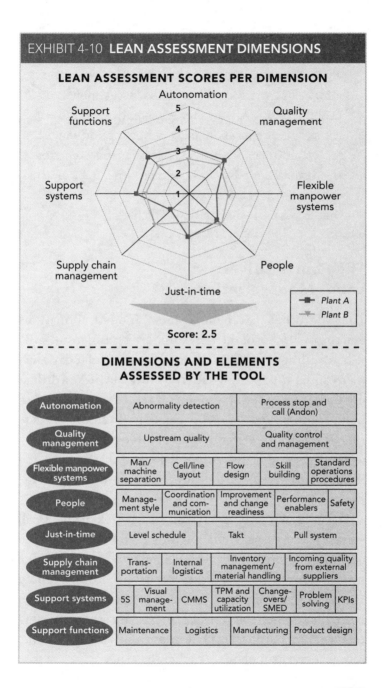

EXHIBIT 4-10 LEAN ASSESSMENT DIMENSIONS

LEAN ASSESSMENT SCORES PER DIMENSION

Autonomation
5
4
3
2
1

Support functions

Quality management

Support systems

Flexible manpower systems

Supply chain management

People

Just-in-time

■ Plant A
▼ Plant B

Score: 2.5

DIMENSIONS AND ELEMENTS ASSESSED BY THE TOOL

Dimension	Elements				
Autonomation	Abnormality detection		Process stop and call (Andon)		
Quality management	Upstream quality		Quality control and management		
Flexible manpower systems	Man/machine separation	Cell/line layout	Flow design	Skill building	Standard operations procedures
People	Management style	Coordination and communication	Improvement and change readiness	Performance enablers	Safety
Just-in-time	Level schedule		Takt	Pull system	
Supply chain management	Transportation	Internal logistics	Inventory management/material handling	Incoming quality from external suppliers	
Support systems	5S, Visual management, CMMS	TPM and capacity utilization	Change-overs/SMED	Problem solving	KPIs
Support functions	Maintenance	Logistics	Manufacturing	Product design	

team of lean experts interacts with line operators and management in a series of shop-floor visits and interviews. Apart from the scores, assessments reveal the best practices that are already embedded within the organization and the best opportunities for immediate improvement. Plant managers tend to overestimate the leanness of their operations, and without an objective standard, gaining consensus on the status quo can be terribly difficult.

The Fourth Driver: Labor Modernization

The sad truth is that in most plants, industrial relations and the treatment of the workforce are reminiscent of the nineteenth century. The cutting-edge ideas of today's human capital and learning experts, proven to make a difference wherever they are implemented, have rarely taken hold. There are indicators, in fact, that conditions are getting worse. In one aerospace plant, three generations have worked on the shop floor since 1945, and absenteeism and illness rates have risen a steady 2 percent in each generation.

Overall, Western manufacturers have taken only small steps toward successfully aligning factory workers with corporate interests. For instance, only 20 percent of the production workers in Western Europe and the United States receive compensation linked to performance, and more than 75 percent work under a salary system so rigid that workers purposely create opportunities for overtime as a necessary supplement to their base pay.

The fundamental need for more effective and humane systems of workforce management is clear and virtually universal in manufacturing. The improvement of labor practices and customization of human resource policies are essential to developing creative and motivated employees. But the most appropriate methods for accomplishing these tasks are decidedly situation-specific. Labor issues vary significantly from one place to another. Workforces in different locales have unique cultures, calendars, family structures, community resources, demographics, education levels, and assumptions about work.

Over the years, manufacturers have experimented with a wide variety of means for engaging shop floor employees. One Dutch chemical company gained the trust of its workforce by guaranteeing the quality of the work environment: it promised not to cut budgets for workspace, maintenance, and modernization. Some companies design and build their plants with the employee experience in mind. Volkswagen's Gläserne Manufaktur in Dresden embraced wood floors, acoustic effects, and avant garde design in an attempt to enhance its products and production process. Surprisingly, the most worker-friendly plant environments in terms of layout, architecture, lighting, and facilities are most often found in older, established plants. Examples include the European plants of Airbus parent company EADS (Exhibit 4-11), which feature a transparent roof design that brings the outdoors in. Botanical gardens on the factory grounds belie the production-based nature of the work going on within. In new plants, the well-being of shop floor communities and ergonomic principles are all too rarely a significant design element.

EXHIBIT 4-11 WELCOMING TO WORKERS: AN EADS PLANT

Source: *Photo courtesy of Getty Images*

The Brazilian cosmetics company Natura has also created an inviting factory "campus," which management believes has bolstered its productivity levels. Angela Cristina Pinhati, industrial and infrastructure manager, says:

> We are concerned about the quality of our workers' lives and the benefits of working for Natura are significant in wages and day-to-day practices on the shop floor. Our buildings are very open, with lots of windows on beautiful grounds and clean environments with a lot of open space. It is important to us that there is a lot of natural light in the shop floor fa-

cilities. Gyms, hairdressers, a medical center are on site—everyone from a doctor to an acupuncturist. We also have a childcare unit that workers can use for three or four years. And we have diversity policies, including quotas for the number of local residents that must be hired and programs for hiring women and people of diverse races. As a result, we have low absenteeism for the region, about or below 3 percent, which is artificially elevated by the days that we give workers off as a freebie—such as their birthdays or a day that they are giving blood.

Another subtle way to enhance life in the factory is to improve the balance of male and female employees. Studies have shown that workplaces that have both men and women working together tend to be perceived as warmer, more fulfilling places. We have heard operations executives confirm this point anecdotally. "Asking all-male production groups to implement a better workplace organization," said one, "is like entering a fraternity house and demanding that they wash their dishes immediately after use. Just forget it." Experience in the most exacting plants—pharmaceutical plants and manufacturing environments like Renault's tractor assembly facilities in Le Mans, France—has also shown that shifts or sections with higher proportions of women as operators tend to meet higher quality standards. Whatever the reason, the multiple advantages of mixed-gender manufacturing workplaces are clear.

Finally, some forward-thinking companies are working hard to overcome the inherent isolation of factories through the development of community and customer relations. Danone, Johnson & Johnson, Procter & Gamble, Harley-Davidson, Mercedes-Benz, and recently BMW all are including their plants in word-of-mouth and face-to-face sales, marketing, and public relations programs. Mercedes, for example, encourages customer-to-factory interaction by suggesting that car buyers pick up their new vehicles at its plant in Sindelfingen, Germany. There, car buyers are encouraged to talk to plant workers about quality and other issues pertaining to their automobiles. And Johnson & Johnson advertises its manufacturing staff and their commitment to quality in its television commercials.

Labor modernization can represent a daunting challenge for manufacturers. In brownfield sites, history often works against change-minded managers. A brownfield workforce is generally older and may have already lived through traumatic events, such as shutdowns, layoffs, and safety incidents, as well as repeated failures of major change initiatives. Unions also have long, often bitter memories of prior plant management teams and can be very reluctant to forge new alliances. Greenfield sites have their labor modernization challenges, too. Enlightened human resources policies do not spring up on their own. This is why companies such as Toyota and Nissan make substantial investments in "soft" elements, such as mentors and training, immediately before and during new plant start-ups.

There are innumerable programs, tools, techniques, and tactics for creating vibrant plant workforces, but they are all based on four basic principles for managing labor relations:

First, treat workers with respect. This doesn't mean hanging banners on factory walls or enlisting the CEO to walk the plant floor once each month; it means demonstrating genuine concern and support for the welfare of employees.

General Motors has a long and contentious history in labor relations, but it recently launched a safety blitz aimed at eliminating accidents in its factories. GM management's commitment and financial support for this program has not gone unnoticed by the company's workers. They have openly expressed real appreciation for the automaker's efforts, a sentiment that may translate over time into increased loyalty and productivity.

Toyota, too, demonstrates its concern for the safety of its workers. In its plants, accidents and near accidents are openly discussed and systematic problem-solving techniques are applied to avoiding them in the future. In addition, at shift meetings, workers are regularly asked to identify safety concerns and possible solutions, a tactic that keeps this issue uppermost in people's minds.

Second, dispassionately recognize the impact of labor unions in your plant, and develop a policy that reduces union opposition. This may mean working to avoid unions altogether, or it may mean finding common ground or simply keeping promises and maintaining enough of a moral high ground so that unions cannot oppose the reforms you make on principle.

LABOR UNIONS AND THE "MAKE OR BREAK" FUTURE

The history of labor relations is contentious and diverse; sometimes, labor unions have been full-fledged partners in the revitalization of manufacturing, and at other times they have been destructive forces. Many farsighted manufacturers have simplified their efforts by avoiding labor unions entirely. There are no unions in Toyota, Honda, or Nissan plants in the United States, for example. But this path, to be sustained, requires treating employees with respect and making it clear that their interests are reasonably well aligned with those of the company. Some manufacturers have bolstered their efforts to improve labor relations by forming partnerships with labor unions. The famous "Scanlon Plan," an innovative approach to manufacturing governance, involved labor unions in managing factories and made them accountable for results.

In most contemporary situations that we know of, unfortunately, the role of the union has been destructive to higher-quality manufacturing. Union leaders often actively impede the efforts of workers to take responsibility for improving their own plants' conditions and performance. Union elections, like many political elections, are often won by accentuating simplistic resentment of the "enemy," which in this case is often the management purveyors of manufacturing reform. And the "work rules" in place in many companies, in which only certain people are allowed to do certain jobs, have had a pernicious effect; they make it difficult for people to learn, build their skills, or contribute beyond the bounds of their narrow job description, and they generally make unionized companies less competitive. Furthermore, the seniority rules that are put in place by many unions are in complete opposition to the lean principles of standardized work, stability, and process ownership.

Some labor leaders have embraced lean or quality principles. In the 1980s, some United Auto Workers leaders met regularly with quality pioneer W. Edwards Deming, and in the early 1990s, Germany's IG Metall Union explored lean concepts, such as teamwork, in a very constructive fashion. However, most of these efforts bogged down because of so-called conflicts of interest. Generally speaking, most industrial unions still have a long way to go in realizing the extent to which their interests coincide with manufacturing's vitality.

In fairness, manufacturing managers have their own history of destructive labor relations, and sometimes labor leaders do have a point in charging that "lean" initiatives are just an excuse for reducing headcount or closing plants. Moreover, as we've seen in this book, those initiatives are generally poorly designed.

How, then, might a unionized company move toward a "make," rather than a "break," future? Some will see their labor unions as opponents and act accordingly. Others will seek to enlist the union as an ally, for there are significant ways in which labor and management agree. Both want a stable long-term future. Both want a safe, congenial, and high-quality workplace. Both want to be proud of their products. Is there a way to raise these mutual goals and reduce the problematic rules? The answer depends on the circumstances of each company, but it is in the interest of both labor and management to find an answer in the affirmative.

Third, develop caring leaders. Uncaring leaders are a historic and continuing source of employee discontent. In contrast, empathetic and concerned leaders win greater levels of commitment, support, and performance from employees.

It's also extremely important to develop leadership from within. Internal development strategies create upward mobility in plants and improve worker skills. Coaching, training, in-depth appraisals, and one-on-one development programs ensure that there are internal candidates for top jobs as those positions become available.

Fourth, systematically reward great performance within plant communities. Top-flight plant management and factory productivity should be supported by programs that publicly celebrate this excellence. These might include incentive systems, rewards for people who learn new skills, or in-depth financial literacy programs that incorporate employee stock ownership plans.

THE LEADERSHIP DILEMMA

The final prerequisite for making it in the future of manufacturing is the right leadership. The formidable changes—significant budgetary requirements and cross-functional management issues—required to make manufacturing work again demand that CEOs be the champions of these efforts. Nevertheless, the final accountability for planning and implementation of a manufacturing strategy will virtually always fall to the chief manufacturing executive. And it is this individual who must present the "make or break" case—the case for investing hearts, minds, and money in manufacturing—to senior management and corporate boards.

In a 2006 study of the attitudes of manufacturing heads from more than 50 companies in Europe, the United States, and South America, we learned that these executives face a common set of leadership challenges. They must maintain a delicate balance between competing priorities—focusing on the direct needs of plant management, addressing the broader issues of optimizing assets, coordinating with other functions, and determining manufacturing's role within the corporation—all at the same time. They rarely have sufficient time to dig into the fundamental causes of their day-to-day problems, which exacerbates those short-term concerns and leaves even less time for long-term planning. And finally, they typically do not have the data and analytics they need for effective strategic decision making.

Beyond these challenges, the similarities between manufacturing leaders end. The study revealed that there is no established model for the position or its reach and purview. In fact, the backgrounds, skill sets, responsibilities, and priorities of the heads of manufacturing varied so widely that it was hard to establish patterns even within a single industry.

Manufacturing's reporting lines between plants and headquarters vary, too. Two-thirds of respondents reported that direct responsibility for manufacturing facilities resided with a COO or a senior executive dedicated to the function. Reporting lines for the rest were split among business unit general managers and country or regional executives.

As a general rule, manufacturing seems to work best when plant managers report to a chief manufacturing officer with centralized oversight. But when plants solely serve local markets, reporting lines from local plants to regional business or division heads often appear.

This local reporting approach can be dangerous if it spawns provincialism and impedes network-level transformations. This recently happened to a specialty steelmaker that invested tens of millions of euros in a program aimed at improving quality and delivery performance to bolster the firm's position against low-cost competitors. The company failed to adjust the organizational chart, leaving regional heads in charge of plant managers. As a result, virtually every attempt to transform the factories was met with passive resistance from local chiefs who either feared losing control of their fiefdoms or worried about the effect of the transformation on their short-term performance.

The range and reach of the manufacturing chief's job varies, too—even within industries. In aerospace, Airbus's manufacturing SVP is responsible only for core manufacturing functions, whereas some of his peers in other companies are responsible for manufacturing and the supply chain, including procurement. In pharmaceuticals, one Pfizer SVP is solely in charge of manufacturing, whereas his equivalent at Novartis also has all of the technical functions under his wing. In food products, Cadbury has regional manufacturing SVPs, whereas others in the industry have local manufacturing chiefs.

Exhibit 4-12 shows that, regardless of who oversees the manufacturing function, it's likely that manufacturing is just one item on his or her agenda. Manufacturing executives can be responsible for product R&D, process R&D, sourcing, supply chain planning, logistics and distribution, sales and marketing, and customer service—as well as human resources, accounting and finance, information technology, and order management!

As the role of the chief manufacturer has broadened, so has the career profile of manufacturing leaders. Historically, manufacturing executives often were promoted from the shop floor or had technical backgrounds. Today, more and more companies are purposely hiring manufacturing leaders who have a broader range of experience, including stints in marketing or finance. A more eclectic background helps ensure that these executives see the big picture rather than fall prey to tunnel vision.

Further, as more and more companies realize the complexities involved in manufacturing transformations, more are hiring manufacturing executives from outside their ranks and industries in the hope that they will bring proven solutions with them. This is also happening in industries that traditionally tended not to hire outside their industries for technical reasons. The chief manufacturing officer at Novartis, for example, comes from the automotive industry, as does the senior manufacturing executive at Airbus.

In the case of a leading European manufacturer of

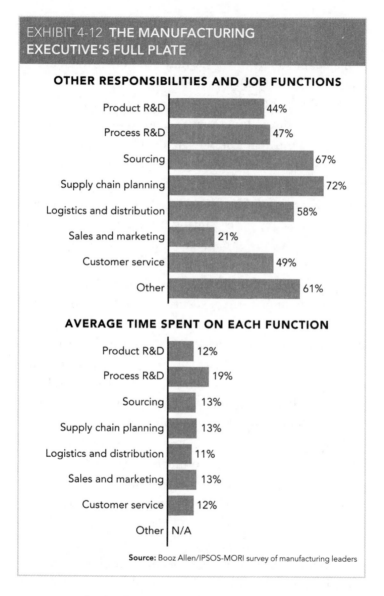

EXHIBIT 4-12 **THE MANUFACTURING EXECUTIVE'S FULL PLATE**

OTHER RESPONSIBILITIES AND JOB FUNCTIONS

- Product R&D — 44%
- Process R&D — 47%
- Sourcing — 67%
- Supply chain planning — 72%
- Logistics and distribution — 58%
- Sales and marketing — 21%
- Customer service — 49%
- Other — 61%

AVERAGE TIME SPENT ON EACH FUNCTION

- Product R&D — 12%
- Process R&D — 19%
- Sourcing — 13%
- Supply chain planning — 13%
- Logistics and distribution — 11%
- Sales and marketing — 13%
- Customer service — 12%
- Other — N/A

Source: Booz Allen/IPSOS-MORI survey of manufacturing leaders

commercial vehicles, a former sales and marketing executive assigned to manufacturing shook up the status quo. He
asked customer-centric questions around order delivery,

customization, and price. The executive encouraged plant management teams to reconsider every routine and detail of the production process and every element of customization in components and the design of vehicles. The result was a redesign of the production system that included new plant layouts, materials and material flows, work processes, and targets. This ultimately evolved into a sustained transformation program driven by market needs and resulted in substantial competitive cost advantages.

Of course, a cross-functional background is not a silver bullet. But generally speaking, the broader the background of manufacturing leaders, the greater the likelihood that their judgment and decisions will be robust and holistic.

Among the many pressures faced by manufacturing heads, the pressure to produce accelerated results tops the list. In the 2006 study cited above, 82 percent of respondents said their superiors demanded that any large investment in manufacturing must produce positive returns within too short a timeframe. Roughly half of these respondents believed that they needed an average of one year

A leading Latin American beer brewer turns its manufacturing leaders into deliverymen in an effort to counter functional isolation and encourage a more customer-centric mind-set. One day each year, every manufacturing executive teams up with a salesperson and rides in a delivery truck as it makes its rounds to distributors and retailers. The executives get into the market and, through informal conversations with customers, get firsthand accounts of their needs, problems, and desires.

longer and the rest said they needed two years more. It is very surprising to find so many seasoned executives with high-level responsibilities struggling with such unrealistic expectations.

To counter this pressure, production chiefs must emerge from their functional silos and create realistic expectations about the value and demands of long-term strategic change. Indeed, a realistic approach to manufacturing, supported by the company's top leaders, can transform an entire organization. In one case, involving an American aluminum company, the company sent an international group of manufacturing and commercial executives to travel around the world benchmarking and collecting best practices. Their findings were translated into a proprietary production system based on lean manufacturing and a judicious mix of total quality management, Six Sigma, and other traditional quality improvement tools, which in turn has been expanded into a company-wide business system. But this work takes time: the initiative is still being refined and improved. Insiders estimate that the entire job will take approximately 10 years.

Even if manufacturing transformations were to have the time and funding needed to achieve success, manufacturing chiefs would not always see the outcomes. Exhibit 4-13 shows that 65 percent of them do not stay in their jobs long enough to complete the typical systemic transformation initiative.

Unfortunately, the pressure for results and the short tenures of manufacturing chiefs usually result in a dearth of strategic decision making. Within manufacturing, strategy formulation is too often seen as a discrete process scheduled once every three years instead of as an ongoing,

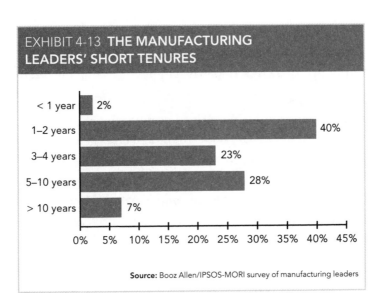

EXHIBIT 4-13 THE MANUFACTURING LEADERS' SHORT TENURES

- < 1 year: 2%
- 1–2 years: 40%
- 3–4 years: 23%
- 5–10 years: 28%
- > 10 years: 7%

Source: Booz Allen/IPSOS-MORI survey of manufacturing leaders

reflective inquiry into the state of the business, the position of competitors, and the emergence of innovative approaches to improving performance.

How manufacturing chiefs spend their time also has a major impact on their ability to lead the kinds of efforts needed to make it in the coming years. Currently their most time-consuming activity is internal meetings, which eat up 27 percent of their work lives. By contrast, only 13 percent of their time is spent with suppliers, customers, unions, and other third parties. These percentages need to flip if manufacturing is to become more agile and responsive. Time spent with suppliers, customers, and competitors can be a significant source of intelligence and insight. More manufacturing executives should be following the lead of the European chemical company that consulted with its major customers before deciding whether to commence operations in China.

Although there is no fixed set of personal characteristics for manufacturing executives in the future, there certainly are qualities that will support and enable their success:

➤ The new manufacturing leader must have the curiosity and passion to cover both "big-M" issues, such as strategic planning, supply chain management, product design, capacity management, interplant coordination, and workforce organization, *and* "small-M" issues, such as cutting, shaping, grinding, assembling, and painting.

➤ The well-rounded leader of the corporate engine room must have the holistic business perspective needed to understand and adjust the role of manufacturing in the context of the broader strategic needs of the company.

➤ The new head of manufacturing must be a skilled advocate who can convince members of the senior leadership team to immerse themselves in the function and better understand it, as well as muster their support.

To those manufacturing organizations that are lucky enough to find such leaders, we offer three words of advice: Give them time.

NATURA TAKES ON THE CHALLENGE

In this interview with Angela Cristina Pinhati, the industrial and infrastructure manager of Natura Cosméticos S/A, we can see the transition in process as a company moves to establish itself as a global manufacturer. Natura, founded in 1969, is Brazil's leading maker of skin care, perfume, and hair care products, priding itself on environmentally friendly products and continual innovation. As shown in this interview, the path to manufacturing leadership is not easy— but the path can be taken, and virtuous cycles can be gradually set in motion.

What is Natura's manufacturing strategy?

Pinhati: We just have one main production site in Brazil, where we manufacture all of our product lines. Natura´s mission is to use the wealth of resources of the Amazon in an exemplary and sustainable fashion. So, Natura will probably always manufacture in Brazil.

But we know that at some point it will not be possible to produce all of our products in a Brazilian site and distribute to all of the markets we want to be in. At that juncture, we would like to have a partner who is willing to invest with us outside of the country, a partner that could open a factory in the European Union or United States, in which we would have a shared investment, to produce products for the local market. But we know it won't be easy to find a large enough company that has capacity to join with us to implement this strategy.

In the past, manufacturing contracting was led by different sourcing areas and wasn't coordinated enough. As a result, we outsourced only to make up for production constraints, and each product team decided themselves whether to outsource. Soon, however, this will be done by committee to elevate the elements of this discussion.

This year, we have developed a new strategy for our outsourcing decisions, based on a long-term perspective and structural drivers. Under this new approach, we prefer not to do any production outside of Brazil on our own. We will look for partners that will help us in the countries we want to enter in the next 10 years.

On the other hand, we won't outsource manufacturing that strategically is critical to Natura's performance. For more complex products, like moisture creams and makeups, we need unique innovation in design and manufacturing, and so we will continue to create, launch, and at least initially produce these items internally—even in the future. We deem these products more complex because they are harder to scale up; they bring a level of complexity to the supply chain since they are made of natural ingredients from forests and fields; and they are often an emotional purchase for which people have very specific preferences. Our outsourcing strategy will be implemented for less complex products, like soap. For items like that, we can get the same output from third parties.

What is Natura's attitude toward lean systems?
Pinhati: Lean processes are tough to implement, especially embedding lean systems in an old existing site with old ways of doing things.

We do not have plans for the complete implementation of lean systems in Natura yet. We do not have the manufacturing strength and established manufacturing operations to consider adopting lean in some total fashion. Two years ago, we started *total productive maintenance* (TPM) (a management system involving systematic equipment maintenance in part driven by input from employees at all levels to improve productivity and minimize downtime). Our goal was to maximize the effectiveness of one selected part of a production system, and we want to finish that successfully first before moving on to the next step deeper into lean systems. Today, we are getting a lot of lean benefits just by doing things smartly—not necessarily by calling it "lean." We think we have an opportunity sometime in the future to implement lean tools more comprehensively to improve lead times and supply chain efficiency. It's not a high priority, but it could be of value in the future.

What do you believe Natura can do to improve the value it gets from manufacturing?

Pinhati: Internally we need the manufacturing function to work more closely with the innovation leaders. Sometimes you can improve plant productivity a great deal with a few small product or process innovations. To manufacture most of our product lines requires a lot of manual work. I still have lines with 15 or 18 people doing manual work. But it is difficult to manage all of these people, to keep them motivated in very repetitive jobs. Because of this we need to invest in automation to handle the simple, mundane jobs so we can raise the skill level of our average

workers and have them oversee more technical operations involving sophisticated machinery and more
advanced production systems.

And while our focus will naturally be on investing
in technology to reduce the repetitive kinds of work,
we must not forget to invest in technology that improves factory processes. We must create a balance
so that technology helps the workers and also helps
achieve the productivity that the company needs.
But there's another trade-off to consider as well:
sometimes automation is difficult to implement and,
thus, not worth the effort. If you go from a human
system to a nonhuman system, you may become less
flexible and lose some of what makes your factory
stand out. All of these are trade-offs, and balances
must be factored in.

Currently, much of our innovation is focused on
marketing, but there is so much innovation possible
in the supply chain that we are now starting to take
advantage of. For example, we should work with our
suppliers to improve the packaging they provide us
with, and to fine-tune the specifications through better technology so there is a lower range of variations
and much less waste. This type of innovation is difficult because other departments or suppliers resist it;
they don't see it as something that is going to produce results. Instead, they see it as an impediment
that will lengthen time to launch a new product. It will
be hard to change this; it will be difficult to get all the
required people to adopt manufacturing innovation.

What is the proper role for the manufacturing executive in the future?

Pinhati: It depends very much on the company's sector. For example, companies whose main products are commodities sold in mass markets will have manufacturing executives whose jobs are critical due to the high impact of supply chain costs. On the other hand, in those companies in which production costs are a lower percentage of the total and in which innovation is more rampant, manufacturing executives will still have an important role, but they will "compete" more with commercial executives.

MAKING A WINNING FUTURE

As the weaknesses of many companies are increasingly exposed, the future of manufacturing is truly becoming a make-or-break proposition. At the same time, there are always great opportunities in challenging times.

Those companies that place a renewed and revitalized focus on a mix of innovative manufacturing process technology, flexible global footprints, deliberately redesigned manufacturing operating systems, and truly engaged manufacturing communities will not simply make winning futures for themselves and their industries—they may change the world. That, after all, is what manufacturers have done since the industrial revolution—indeed, throughout human history.

The aim of this book has been to create a portrait of what companies will have to do to play a leading role in the future. Those companies that succeed will ignite internal investment and enthusiasm for manufacturing, as well as raise and meet senior management's expectations for the function. They will hire manufacturing talent with the same diligence and urgency that goes into filling strategy, product development, and marketing positions. They will promote products and processes that are more environmentally benign, more friendly to workers and neighbors, and more flexible than those of the past. They will transform the manufacturing culture while aggressively and rigorously pursuing both incremental and breakthrough levels of innovation in process technology and manufacturing footprints. They may well achieve lasting positions for their companies that financial or market crises cannot dislodge.

While there are many factors beyond manufacturing that affect financial results and equity valuation, if the track record of great manufacturers is an accurate indicator of performance, then the manufacturing leaders of tomorrow will also deliver returns that are far above average. To accomplish this, they will reject the conventional view of manufacturing as a pure cost center, which leads to an exaggerated reluctance to invest. Instead, they will view manufacturing from an *extended-value* perspective that fully considers the potential return on manufacturing, including

➤ The value of bottom-line improvements beyond fair performance expectations in today's operational setup

➤ The value of increased top-line improvements in price realization and increased sales with today's operational setup

➤ The value that will accrue when manufacturing delivers defensible competitive advantages because of step-changes in the operational setup

This perspective will enable these companies to raise the bar and their aspirations for manufacturing to new heights.

To achieve competitive advantage through manufacturing, winning companies will also require a comprehensive manufacturing strategy that delineates a clear and compelling path to a successful future. They will act decisively, using a mix of long-term initiatives and near-term improvements to create the confidence and patience required to achieve manufacturing excellence.

The time to capture a winning future in manufacturing is roughly *now*. This is the "make-or-break" moment: the time to create a strategic plan that encompasses the present and the future, that negates the mistakes of the past, that rides on waves of innovation, and that counts making something—or, better yet, making something extraordinary—as a very credible and worthwhile use of a company's time.

For notes and resources visit our Web site:
www.businessfuture.com

INDEX

ABOUT THE AUTHORS

KAJ GRICHNIK is a vice president of Booz Allen Hamilton, and a specialist in manufacturing transformations. Based in Munich, he previously worked for CRL, a supplier to the pharma industry. He holds master's degrees in geology and microeconomics, and an MBA degree from the MIT Sloan School of Management. Kaj is the lead author of *Manufacturing Realities: Breaking the Boundaries of Conventional Practice* (*strategy+business* books, 2006) and a frequent contributor to *strategy+business* and other publications.

CONRAD WINKLER is a vice president of Booz Allen Hamilton, based in Chicago, and an expert in manufacturing strategy, manufacturing transformation, and supply chain management. He was previously a nuclear submariner in the U.S. Navy. He holds an MBA from Northwestern University's Masters of Management in Manufacturing program (a joint program between the Kellogg Graduate School of Management and the McCormick School of Engineering and Applied Sciences), and a BS in mechanical engineering from Massachusetts Institute of Technology. He is a long-standing contributor to *strategy+ business* on manufacturing, supply chain, and other operations-related topics.

JEFFREY ROTHFEDER is a senior editor at *strategy+business*, and a veteran business journalist and editor. He is the author of several books, including *McIlhenny's Gold: How a Louisiana Family Built the Tobasco Empire* (Collins, 2007). He is also the editor of *Manufacturing Realities* (*strategy+ business* books, 2006) and *The Missing Link* (*strategy+business* books, 2005).

In researching, writing, and editing this book, the authors drew upon the advice, knowledge, and experience of a number of colleagues at our global management consulting firm. They include the following:

NAVNEET ARORA is a senior associate based in Chicago. A specialist in manufacturing strategy and sourcing, he worked previously for the Dow Chemical Company and has consulted across several industries, including automotive, health care, and consumer products.

MATTHIAS BAEUMLER is a principal based in Berlin. He specializes in operations and R&D strategy as well as supply chain improvement in the global chemicals and pharmaceuticals industries. Prior to his current position, he worked for BASF.

CHRISTIAN BASEDOW, an associate based in Munich, specializes in manufacturing brownfield transformations and supply chain management, with a particular focus on process industries, and has extensive experience in Germany and South Africa. He previously worked for Lurgi AG, the factory engineering company.

HANNES BEHACKER, an associate based in Berlin, is an expert in supply chain and manufacturing across a variety of industries, including chemicals, pharmaceuticals, aeronautics, and consumer goods. His background includes work for international firms in China and Russia.

HANS BOHNEN, a senior associate, has significant experience leading business excellence programs, and in operational and commercial improvement transformations for the pharmaceutical, chemical, and manufacturing industries. Based in Dusseldorf, he was previously employed by Hoechst AG, Celanese AG, and SGL Group, where he headed the global lean Six Sigma program.

ERIC DUSTMAN, a principal with the firm, is based in Chicago. A specialist in manufacturing and supply chain operations, he was previously employed by Motorola.

AMIT GAUTAM is an associate based in Amsterdam. An expert in product design, manufacturing strategy, and in-plant cost reduction, he previously worked for General Electric Aircraft Engines.

GEORGINA GRENON, director of the firm's global business development and intellectual capital efforts in operations, manufacturing, sourcing, and logistics, is based in Paris. She has recently led an ongoing initiative in energy-efficient and sustainable supply chain management and sourcing. She oversaw the research, development, and promotion of this book.

DOUGLAS HARDMAN is a vice president based in Chicago. He specializes in operations strategy, designing and implementing new operating models, and supply chain management and was formerly employed by Electrolux's U.S. subsidiary, Frigidaire.

PETER VON HOCHBERG is a vice president based in Dusseldorf. He has deep expertise in operations with a special focus on the automotive and industrial sectors and strong experience in lean manufacturing. With over 20 years of consulting experience, he has advised major industry clients around the globe on manufacturing challenges.

KEN HOGAN is a senior associate, based in Detroit, who works with automobile and industrial companies to develop manufacturing strategies and analyze competitive cost positions. He was formerly employed by Detroit Diesel Corporation.

THORNTON HUGHES is an associate based in Chicago who specializes in manufacturing strategy for automotive and aerospace companies. He previously worked for Ford Motor Company and Moog Incorporated.

ARVIND KAUSHAL, a principal based in Chicago, is an expert in manufacturing strategy and competitive cost assessment. He focuses on the automotive, industrial, and building products industries.

IAN MACDONALD, an associate in the New York office, specializes in supply chain management and served as interim acting director for this book. He previously worked at Boeing.

MARCUS MORAWIETZ is a principal based in the Frankfurt office. He focuses on operations strategy and supply chain performance improvement, primarily in the global chemical and pharmaceutical industries. He previously worked for Degussa (now Evonik), a specialty chemical company.

JERÔME PELLAN, a senior associate based in Paris, specializes in manufacturing and engineering management for the automotive and industrials sectors. He has previously worked for Renault, Nissan, and Volvo Trucks.

JOHN POTTER, a vice president located in London, is an expert in operations strategy, supply chain, and manufacturing management. His previous employer was the U.S. Navy.

ASHISH RANJAN is an associate with expertise in lean Six Sigma based enterprise-transformation, value stream restructuring, and process redesign, with a special focus on the aerospace and automotive industries. Located in London, he previously worked for Tata Motors, India, in its Lean Transformation program.

DERMOT SHORTEN is a vice president based in New York, who specializes in end-to-end supply chain design and performance improvement. He was previously employed at Deloitte Haskins + Sells.

CAROLINE THIEDIG, an associate based in Berlin, specializes in manufacturing and supply chain management in the process and pharmaceutical industries. She is an expert in production network optimization, operating asset effectiveness, and distribution strategies.

SVEN VALLERIEN is a vice president based in the Dusseldorf office. He is an expert in manufacturing, strategic sourcing, and supply chain management. He formerly worked at Th. Goldschmitt AG (now Evonik), a global specialty chemical company.

CHRISTOPH BLISS, our colleague in Germany and China, made an enormous contribution to the book's research, especially on manufacturing in China. He unexpectedly passed away in Shanghai on December 3, 2007, while this book was being edited. He has been often in our thoughts, and we all have many fond memories of his creativity and zest for life.

For notes to the quotes and citations in this book, and for updated references, see our Web site:
www.businessfuture.com

ACKNOWLEDGMENTS

The "future of business" series has been a collaborative effort from the beginning. Our editor and publisher at McGraw-Hill, Herb Schaffner, has been a wise and enthusiastic guide every step of the way—the model of a business book publisher-editor. We have also benefited from the talents of senior production supervisor Ruth Mannino and the rest of the team at McGraw-Hill.

The book was developed and edited under the auspices of *strategy+business*, the quarterly magazine published by our firm, and some parts of it appeared first in *s+b*'s pages. We would like to thank the entire *s+b* team, and, in particular, publisher Jonathan Gage, who helped conceive the project and moved it along at every stage; managing editor Elizabeth Johnson, who stepped in to help with the difficult problem of locating permissions for images; literary agent Jim Levine, who helped make the book possible; and publicist Mark Fortier and marketing manager Alan Shapiro, who have helped make the book visible. Senior editor Ted Kinni was the linchpin who provided editorial oversight and clarity. Art Kleiner, editor-in-chief of *strategy+ business* (and in our view a living encyclopedia of management theory), was involved in the project from conception to final edit, and contributed to many of the ideas and approaches that made the book work.

Our colleagues at the firm have given us the encouragement and support we needed to bring excellence to this project. As part of the "intellectual capital engine," this project benefited from a platform of support and collaborative thought that is rare in any enterprise. We particularly wish to thank Ron Haddock, Peter Heckmann, William Jackson, Barry Jaruzelski, Cesare Mainardi, and Keith Oliver.

Our friends at RWD—quite likely the world's leading lean implementation boutique and our preferred partner in manufacturing transformations—have contributed to this book in great measure. We particularly benefited from the perspective, creativity, and good will of Simon Castleman, John Kelly, Mike Olive, Jim Parish, Will Seager, and Mike Turner, who have more than 150 years of combined experience in lean manufacturing and other forms of enlightened operations, including much experience at Toyota.

Many of the real life and firsthand examples in this book have been made possible by the generous contribution and openness of executives from leading manufacturing companies. We want to especially thank Keith Harrison and Paul Fox from Procter & Gamble, Angela Pinhati and Marcello Rodrigues from Natura, Michel Lurquin from UCB, Thierry Chiche from Michelin, Rich Forbes and Greg Stoner from Fortune Brands/MasterBrand Cabinets, and Tom Burke from Modine Manufacturing Company, as well as manufacturing executives from the Tata Group, Lego, Zara, and General Motors.